FROM WORRIES TO WAGS

Tim Shine

Buy Me Now Co.

Copyright © 2023 by Tim Shine
Editor: Nivol Redan
Interior & cover design: Brita Zoland
Publisher: Buy Me Now Co.

Copyright © 2023 by Tim Shine. All rights reserved. This book, or any part thereof, may not be reproduced through any mechanical, photographic, or electronic process or in the form of a phonographic recording. It may not be stored in a retrieval system, transmitted, or copied in any manner for public or private use without author permission.

The content in this book is not intended to serve as medical advice or to advocate for using any technique to treat physical, emotional, or medical issues in dogs without consulting a veterinarian or relevant experts directly or indirectly. The author aims to present general information to assist you and your dogs. Should you choose to apply any information from this book to your dog, exercising your constitutional rights, please be aware that neither the author nor the publisher assumes any responsibility for your actions.

From Worries to Wags, Explore the Dark Side of Dogs' Life / Tim Shine – 1st Edition.
ISBN: 978-0-6458916-0-7
1. Pets / Dogs / Breeds 2. Pets / Dogs / Training & Showing 3. Pets / Reference
Thema: Dogs as pets, World

Prince Award dedicated to Tim Shine by Buy Me Now Co.

The book has now been translated into multiple languages, including Spanish, French, German, Dutch, Italian, Japanese, and Chinese. The decision to translate the book was driven by the overwhelming demand from dog lovers worldwide and the shared goal of securing and protecting the well-being of dogs across the globe. By making this valuable resource accessible to a wider audience, we hope to empower dog owners and enthusiasts from different cultures to provide the best care and understanding for their beloved furry companions and achieve global recognition. Together, let's make a positive impact on the lives of dogs everywhere.

Please use the following ISBN codes to find the respective translations of this book. You can utilize the dedicated code for online searches or present it to bookstores for assistance in locating the desired translations.

Language	**Book name**	**ISBN No**
English	From Worries to Wags	978-0-6458916-0-7
Spanish	De las Preocupaciones a las Movidas de Cola	978-0-6458916-1-4
French	Des Inquiétudes aux Remuements de Queue	978-0-6458916-2-1
Italian	Dalle Preoccupazioni alle Scodinzolate	978-0-6458916-3-8
German	Von Sorgen zu Schwanzwedeln	978-0-6458916-4-5
Dutch	Van Zorgen naar Kwispels	978-0-6458916-5-2
Chinese	从焦虑到摇尾巴	978-0-6458916-6-9
Japanese	心配から尻尾を振ることへ	978-0-6458916-7-6

From Worries to Wags
Explore The Bark Side of Dogs Anxiety Life

A Must-Have Guidebook for Dog Lovers

Table of Contents:

Dedication _____ 11
Author note _____ 13
Acknowledgments _____ 15
Publisher Note _____ 17
Preface _____ 19

Chapter 1: Unleashing the World of Dog Anxiety _____ 21
Understanding the Canine Anxious Mind _____ 21
Exploring the Unique Anxiety Levels in Different Breeds _____ 23

Chapter 2: Decoding the Language of Anxiety _____ 25
Reading My Non-Verbal Cues: Signs and Signals _____ 25
Physical Symptoms of Anxiety: Heart Racing, Tail Tucks, and More __ 26

Chapter 3: Digging into the Root Causes _____ 29
Separation Anxiety: Please Don't Leave Me Alone! _____ 29
Noise Phobias: Fireworks, Thunderstorms, and More _____ 31
Social Anxiety: Making Friends and Overcoming Fears _____ 32
Chapter 2 & 3 summary _____ 34

Chapter 4: Creating a Haven of Calm _____ 35
Designing a Calming Environment: My Safe Sanctuary _____ 35
Positive Reinforcement Training: Paw-sitive Methods for Confidence _ 36
Consistency is Key: Routines to Soothe My Anxious Soul _____ 36

Chapter 5: Paw-some Products to Ease My Anxiety … 39
Cozy Comfort: Exploring the Wonders of ThunderShirts … 39

Engaging Distractions: Interactive Toys for Stress Relief … 40

Chapter 6: When Extra Help is Needed … 43
Medications: A Look into the Options … 43

Seeking Professional Support: Behaviorists and Trainers … 44

Common Dog Diseases … 45

Vaccinations … 50

Chapter 7: Nurturing the Caregiver Within You … 51
Dogs' Hygiene, what we should know … 51

Self-Care for Dog Owners: Finding Balance and Support … 52

Chapter 8: Finding Zen with Your Furry Friend … 55
Embracing Mindfulness … 55

Mindful Moments … 56

Mindful Walks … 58

Creating a Zen Space … 59

Mindful Training … 60

Dog Music … 61

Chapter 9: Training, Tips, and Tricks … 63
Different breeds' training aspects … 63

Sniffing Out the Best … 65

Wag-tastic Classes … 67

Workshops and Seminars … 69

Sources and Tools … 70

Unleashing Your Inner Superhero … 71

Training examples … 72

Chapter 10: General Health & 40 popular breeds anxiety summary ___ 75
Health, Age, Vaccination ___ 75
My Food ___ 76
My Checklist ___ 78
40 Popular breeds anxiety summary ___ 80

Chapter 11: Nap & Walk to stay tuned ___ 103

Chapter 12: Puppy Anxious World ___ 105
My puppy time memory ___ 105
From puppy to an adult dog stage ___ 107
New puppy, pup-to-human advice ___ 108
Puppy challenges and solutions ___ 109

Chapter 13: Last but not least ___ 113
Chapter 14: Each breed detail, your dog's explanatory page ___ 117
Chapter 15: 10 Excellent Websites ___ 199
Chapter 16: Sources and References, Where to Dig Deeper ___ 203

Chapter 17: 10 Super Helpful Comparison Tables ___ 205
40 Popular Breeds Characteristics ___ 206
40 Popular breeds anxiety type, level, and signs ___ 208
40 popular breeds anxiety signs and root causes ___ 212
40 Popular breeds hygiene detail ___ 214
40 popular breeds training aspects ___ 216
40 popular breeds General health and age data ___ 220
40 Popular breeds physiology data ___ 224
40 Popular breeds intelligence levels ___ 226
40 Popular breeds nap, walk, and in/outdoor profile ___ 228
Puppy life stage development ___ 230

Glossary ___ 231
Dog Book Logbook ___ 235

To my compassionate daughter,

This book is dedicated to you, my kindred spirit and advocate for the voiceless. Your endless love for animals always inspires me. May this book be a guiding light, empowering you and others to make a difference in dogs' lives. Thank you for your unwavering compassion.

With boundless love and admiration

Author note

Woof woof! Hey there, I'm a dog, I'm a pug. My name is **Prince**.

In this tail-waggingly comprehensive guide, I, your loyal and loving companion, will lead you on a journey into the intricate world of dog anxiety. Together, we will sniff out the root causes of a dog's anxiety, explore the varying levels in different breeds, and uncover the behaviors that can send my anxiety soaring. Through this adventure, you will gain precious insights into the signs and symptoms of anxiety, allowing you to decipher triggers and truly understand my experiences.

But fret not, dear owner, for I won't leave you hanging! I will arm you with practical strategies to help ease my anxiety and bring peace to my trembling paws. From creating a serene environment to employing positive reinforcement techniques, you will discover the keys to supporting my emotional well-being. And hey, let's not forget about those nifty products that can lend a helping paw in alleviating my worries. We'll dive into a delightful array of anxiety-relieving tools, as well as shed light on medications and professional interventions.

Make sure you don't miss checking out the anxiety summaries of each breed in Chapter 10. And guess what? In Chapter 14, you've got breed-specific pages waiting for your curious eyes. I even fetched some screenshots for you, the real treasure lies in reading those pages. Dive in and let the tail-wagging adventure begin!

Oh, but wait dear owner, I haven't forgotten about you! I understand that my anxiety can tug at your heartstrings and sometimes overwhelm you. That's why I've included a section dedicated to your well-being. I offer guidance on self-care and support, recognizing that your own emotional balance is essential in providing the best care for me. I encourage you to embrace coping strategies and remind you of the importance of seeking help when needed.

By the end of this adventure, you will be equipped with a treasure trove of knowledge and a toolbox bursting with practical tools to guide me towards a happier, more balanced life. Together, we will weave a harmonious bond built on trust, compassion, and understanding.

Remember, this book serves as a general guide and should not replace the advice of professionals. Always consult a veterinarian or certified animal behaviorist for personalized guidance tailored to my unique needs.

So, grab your leash and join me on this journey. Together, we will conquer anxiety and create a world of tail-wagging joy!

With a wag of my tail and a touch of nervous excitement,

Prince
The Anxious Author!

worriestowags@gmail.com

Acknowledgments

Woof! Woof! Tail-wagging greetings to all my amazing companions out there! It's time to give heartfelt thanks to those who helped make this paw-some book a reality. I couldn't share my wisdom with you without their support and love. So, here's a special shout-out to my pack of incredible beings:

First and foremost, a big slobbery lick goes out to my human buddy, who patiently typed my barks into words and brought my canine thoughts to life on these pages. Your paw-some dedication and endless belly rubs kept me motivated throughout this journey.

To my doggy friends, both near and far, you inspire me every day with your wagging tails and unconditional love. Your encouragement lifted my spirits and reminded me that we're together. Let's continue exploring the world with curious noses and joyful bounces!

A wet nose bop to all the veterinarians and animal behaviorists who share their wisdom and expertise. Your dedication to our health and well-being is truly admirable. Your guidance has helped countless pups, and their humans find the path to a happier and more balanced life.

To the publishers and editors, thank you for believing in my book and giving it a chance to shine. Your support and guidance have been invaluable, and I'm forever grateful for the opportunity to share my adventures with the world.

I can't forget to wag my tail and give a paw-five to all the dogs who shared their stories, bringing an extra sprinkle of authenticity to these pages. Your experiences have touched my heart and inspired me to create a book that addresses the fears, anxieties, and triumphs we face as furry beings.

Last but not least, a heartfelt thank you to you, dear reader, for embarking on this journey with me. Your love for our kind and dedication to improving our lives make my tail wag with joy. I hope this book brings you valuable insights, helps you understand us on a deeper level, and strengthens the bond you share with your four-legged companion.

A big thanks to all the talented photographers on **Pixel**, **Pixabay** and **Unsplash** websites for capturing the beauty of my fellow dog breeds. Their amazing photos bring these furry friends to life, allowing us to appreciate their unique characteristics. Each click of the camera showcases the incredible bond between humans and dogs, and I'm grateful for their contributions in sharing the diverse and charming world of dogs. Woof!

Remember, my furry friend, together we can create a world filled with wagging tails, endless snuggles, and an abundance of treats. Stay paw-sitive, embrace the love, and keep spreading the joy wherever you go!

With boundless tail wags and a heart full of gratitude.

Your Furry Author
Prince

Publisher Note

Dear Dog Lover,

Let us introduce you to the remarkable author of this book, **Prince** the Anxious Dog. Prince may be a little bundle of nerves, but don't let that fool you. Prince's experiences and journey with anxiety have given him a unique insight into the world of anxious dogs, making him the perfect voice to guide you through this important topic.

As a publisher, we were captivated by Prince's book and his unwavering determination to make a difference in the lives of anxious dogs and their human companions. We recognized the need for a comprehensive resource that tackles the complexities of dog anxiety while providing practical solutions and genuine understanding.

Prince's authenticity and relatability are what makes this book truly special. Through his own anxieties, he sheds light on the challenges dogs face, helping readers understand the emotions and behaviors that can arise from anxiety. His personal anecdotes and experiences will resonate with both dogs and humans alike, fostering empathy and compassion.

Our team of editors and experts have worked closely with him to ensure that the information provided is accurate, informative, and accessible. We understand the importance of addressing anxiety in dogs, as it can greatly impact their overall well-being and the bond they share with their human companions.

We believe this book will be a valuable resource for dog owners, veterinarians, trainers, and anyone who wants to support their anxious furry friends. Prince's unique perspective, combined with expert advice and practical tips, offers a comprehensive guide that can help create a harmonious and anxiety-free environment for dogs.

This book's achievement target is global recognition, and is now available in multiple languages, including Spanish, French, Dutch, Italian, Japanese, and Chinese. We plan to add more languages to the list. The decision to translate the book was driven by the overwhelming demand from dog lovers worldwide and the shared goal of securing and protecting the well-being of dogs across the globe. By making this valuable resource accessible to a wider audience, we hope to empower dog owners and enthusiasts from different cultures to provide the best care and understanding for their beloved furry companions.

Together, let's positively impact the lives of dogs everywhere. As a publisher, our mission is to amplify voices that make a positive impact, and Prince's hints resonated deeply with us. We are proud to have partnered with Prince to bring this book to life and share his heartfelt message with the world.

Buy Me Now Co.

Preface

A Tail-Wagging Adventure into My Anxiety

Woof woof! Hello, fellow dog fans! I'm **Prince**; let me start…

Imagine you're snuggled up with me, your loyal and loving furry friend. Suddenly, my ears perk up, my tail droops, and a look of unease flashes across my adorable face. You may have wondered, "What's happening in my precious pup's mind? How can I help ease their worries and create a haven?"

Fear not, my human friends! Together, we'll explore the fascinating world of my anxiety, unravel its secrets, and uncover the strategies that will bring me comfort and peace.

Woof! I understand that every dog, like me, is a unique individual. Whether you have a playful Poodle, a regal Retriever, or a mischievous Terrier, this book is tailor-made for us. We'll delve into the anxiety levels experienced by different breeds, allowing you to better understand my specific needs. No more puzzling over why I get anxious during thunderstorms or tremble when faced with new situations.

But wait, there's more! We'll decipher the signs and signals of anxiety I may send you. From my heart racing to those subtle tail tucks and quivering paws, we'll uncover the secret language of my body. By becoming fluent in my non-verbal cues, you'll be better equipped to provide the support and comfort I crave, transforming anxious moments into courage and confidence.

Woof woof! Now let's dig into the root causes of my anxiety. We'll explore everything from separation anxiety (please don't leave me alone!) to noise phobias (fireworks, anyone?) and social anxiety (time to make new furry friends!). We'll also address the impact of past traumatic experiences and the fears that may linger within me. Together, we'll shed light on the reasons behind my anxious episodes and work towards creating a world where I can feel safe and secure.

Explore the Dark Side of Dogs Life

Preface

Now, let's uncover the magic to reduce my anxiety! I'll share some insider tips on creating a calming environment, using positive reinforcement training techniques, and establishing consistent routines that make me feel as snug as a bug in a rug. We'll sniff out some fantastic products, like cozy ThunderShirts and engaging interactive toys, that can help alleviate my anxiety and bring peace to my doggy heart.

But wait, sometimes a little extra support is needed, and that's okay! We'll embark on a journey into the realm of medications and professional interventions (cue the serious bark). I'll explain when medications might be necessary and introduce you to the incredible behaviorists and trainers who can lend their expertise. We'll ensure I receive the care and support I need to lead a life free from overwhelming anxiety.

Oh, and let's not forget about you, my fantastic human companion! We know that taking care of an anxious dog can be a challenge. That's why we've included a section on self-care and support. We want to ensure you're equipped to nurture your well-being while being the superhero who guides me through the ups and downs of my anxiety-filled world.

So, are you ready to embark on this thrilling adventure into my anxiety? Let's wag our tails, bark excitedly, and turn the pages together! By the end of this book, you'll have gained a deeper understanding of our anxiety, a toolkit of practical tips, and a heart overflowing with love and compassion for your four-legged friend.

By the way, I've made sure that all my furry friends are listed alphabetically in each chapter to make it easier for you to find your paw-some dog. Whether you're exploring the breeds in the chapter about characteristics, health, wellness, or anxiety signs, you can quickly locate the breed you're interested in. No more sniffing around and wasting time!

Flip through the chapters, and you'll discover a treasure trove of information about each delightful breed. So, prepare to embark on your exciting journey to find the perfect companion who will wag their tail and melt your heart.

Happy searching! Woof!

A Must Have Guidebook for Dog Lovers

Chapter 1

From Worries to Wags

Unleashing the World of Dog Anxiety

Understanding the Canine Anxious Mind

Woof woof! Welcome, dear owner, to the thrilling first chapter of our incredible adventure together! It's me, your loyal and lovable furry friend, and I'm here to guide you through the fascinating world of dog anxiety. Although I may not speak your language, I communicate with you through my behaviors and body language. <u>When anxiety takes hold of me, you might notice my tail tucking between my legs, my ears pinned back, or even the subtle tremble in my paws.</u> These are my ways of expressing the unease that grips my heart, and I'm counting on you to be my trusted ally in navigating through it.

To truly understand the intricate workings of the canine anxious mind, we must explore the various factors contributing to my anxiety. Just like humans, I have a unique blend of genetics and life experiences that shape who I am. <u>Some of us dogs are more predisposed to anxiety due to our genetic makeup, while others may have had past experiences that negatively impact our emotional well-being.</u>

But fear not, dear owner! It's not all nature and nurture! The environment in which I live also plays a significant role in determining my anxiety levels. <u>Sudden changes, loud noises, unfamiliar faces, or even your own behavior can trigger anxiety in me.</u> That's why it's crucial for you to create a safe and secure space for me, providing stability and reassurance as we navigate life together.

You, my fantastic human companion, hold the key to unlocking a world of understanding and compassion. You can decipher the language of my anxiety by learning to interpret my subtle cues and signals. When you notice my body tense or my eyes darting around nervously, it's a sign that I need your gentle support and understanding. <u>A soothing touch, a calm voice, and a comforting presence can work wonders in easing my troubled heart.</u>

But it's not just about recognizing my anxiety. It's about delving deeper into the root causes and triggers. Is it the thunderstorms that send shivers down my spine? Or perhaps

Explore the Dark Side of Dogs Life

it's the fear of being separated from you, my cherished companion? By identifying these triggers, we can work together to develop strategies that alleviate my anxiety and help me feel safe and secure.

Remember, dear owner, that your role as my guardian is vital in helping me overcome my fears. Patience, empathy, and consistency are the keys to our success. Together, we'll embark on a journey of gradual exposure, introducing me to the things that cause me anxiety in a controlled and positive manner. This will help me build resilience and confidence, knowing that you're there to protect and guide me every step of the way.

As we continue our adventure, we'll explore many anxiety-related topics, including separation anxiety, noise phobias, and social anxiety. We'll uncover valuable insights from experts in the field, share heartwarming stories of triumph over anxiety, and discover practical techniques to support me on my journey to emotional well-being.

But let me remind you, dear owner, that this journey is not just about me—it's about us. By understanding my anxiety, you'll improve my quality of life, strengthen our bond, and deepen our connection. Together, we'll create a harmonious and loving environment where I can thrive and be the happiest dog by your side.

So, let's embark on this extraordinary adventure, hand in paw, as we unravel the complexities of dog anxiety. I wag my tail excitedly, knowing you're committed to understanding and supporting me. Together, we'll conquer every fear, navigate every challenge, and create a world filled with love, trust, and endless tail-wagging joy.

Exploring the Unique Anxiety Levels in Different Breeds

Let's start by shedding light on one common type of anxiety that affects many of us: separation anxiety. Ah, the familiar pang that fills my heart when you step away from my side. The fear of being alone, separated from the one I love, can be overwhelming. It's not that I don't trust you, dear owner, but rather that I rely on your presence to feel safe and secure. When you leave, a wave of distress washes over me, and it may manifest in destructive behaviors or excessive barking. Remember, your reassurance and patience go a long way in soothing my anxious soul.

A Must Have Guidebook for Dog Lovers

Chapter 1

Now, let's wag our tails over to noise phobia. Picture the crackling thunder during a storm or the explosive booms of fireworks on celebratory occasions. These sudden and intense sounds can send my heart racing and leave me seeking solace and comfort. <u>During these challenging moments, I need your understanding and reassurance.</u> Be my anchor in the face of those scary sounds, providing a calm presence and creating a soothing environment that shields me from the anxiety-inducing noises.

Social anxiety is another hurdle that may weigh heavily on my furry shoulders. Just like some humans, I may feel uneasy or fearful in certain social situations. Meeting unfamiliar dogs or encountering new people can be intimidating for me. <u>It's essential to approach socialization with patience and understanding, allowing me to gradually build confidence and trust in these interactions.</u> With your support, we can overcome my social anxiety and create positive experiences that strengthen my social skills and self-assurance.

Now, let's dig our paws deeper into anxiety levels in different breeds. <u>Each breed carries its own unique set of characteristics, including our predisposition to anxiety.</u> For example, breeds like the Border Collie or the German Shepherd tend to be highly intelligent and sensitive, making us more prone to anxiety. On the other paw, breeds like the Golden Retriever or the Labrador Retriever often exhibit a more easygoing and resilient nature.

<u>However, it's important to remember that anxiety can affect any breed. Generalizations based solely on breed stereotypes may not accurately represent my individual needs and experiences.</u> I am an individual with my own quirks, personality, and sensitivities. Factors such as upbringing, socialization, and overall health also influence my anxiety levels. So, dear owner, approach me with an open heart, ready to understand and support me in a way that is unique to who I am.

By unraveling the depths of the canine anxious mind and exploring the variations in anxiety levels among different breeds, we lay the foundation for a stronger bond and a happier life together. Armed with this knowledge, you can provide the care and support I need to overcome my anxieties, leading to a harmonious and anxiety-free existence.

So, let's continue our thrilling journey, dear owner, as we uncover more secrets and unravel the complexities of dog anxiety. With each page turned, our understanding and connection will deepen, forging an unbreakable bond built on trust, compassion, and love.

Explore the Dark Side of Dogs Life

Stay tuned for the next chapter, where we'll dive into practical strategies and techniques to alleviate anxiety and promote emotional well-being. Together, we'll conquer every obstacle and create a world where anxiety is a thing of the past.

Choosing the right dog breed is a weighty decision that can significantly affect your lifestyle and overall happiness. Understanding the characteristics of different breeds is essential to find the perfect match for your family. I've provided a table in Chapter 17 with detailed information about various dog breeds, including their size, temperament, exercise needs, and compatibility with children or other pets. This comprehensive table allows potential dog owners to make an informed choice that aligns with their preferences and ensures a harmonious and fulfilling relationship with their furry friend. Check out "**40 popular breeds Characteristics.**"

Chapter 2

Decoding the Language of Anxiety

Woof woof! Welcome to the enthralling second chapter of our incredible journey together! It's me again, your loyal and expressive furry friend, ready to help you decipher the complex language of anxiety that I speak. Get ready to dive deep into the world of non-verbal cues and physical symptoms as we explore the depths of my anxious emotions.

Reading My Non-Verbal Cues: Signs and Signals

Dear owner, have you ever wondered what happens inside my furry head when anxiety takes hold of me? Although I cannot communicate with words like you do, I speak to you through my non-verbal cues and behaviors. It's time to sharpen your observation skills and learn to read the subtle signs and signals that reveal the turmoil within.

One of the key indicators of anxiety is my body language. <u>Watch closely for the telltale signs of a tucked tail, ears pinned back, or a lowered head.</u> These are clear signals that I'm feeling uncertain or frightened. When my tail wags low, or my body appears tense, it's a sign that I'm experiencing heightened stress. Please pay attention to these visual cues as they glimpse the storm brewing within my anxious mind.

The eyes, indeed, are the windows to my soul, dear owner. Observe my gaze to gain insight into my emotional state. <u>Dilated pupils may indicate fear or anxiety, while avoiding direct eye contact might be my way of showing submission or discomfort. Additionally, excessive panting or yawning can signify unease and serve as a plea for your support and reassurance.</u> These non-verbal cues are my desperate attempt to convey my inner struggles.

Explore the Dark Side of Dogs Life

Decoding the Language of Anxiety

In moments of anxiety, you might witness me engaging in displacement behaviors. These behaviors are my way of coping with the overwhelming emotions I'm experiencing. You may see me licking my lips, scratching excessively, or shaking off as if to shake my worries away. <u>Though they may seem unrelated, these actions temporarily release my tension.</u> By recognizing these displacement behaviors, you can understand the depth of my anxiety and offer the comfort and understanding I so desperately seek.

Remember, dear owner, understanding my non-verbal cues is crucial to helping me feel safe and secure. By reading my body language, you can offer the comfort and support I need during those anxious moments. Your ability to interpret my signals allows us to deepen our connection and navigate the complexities of anxiety together.

The next chapter explores practical strategies and techniques to help alleviate anxiety and promote my emotional well-being. Stay by my side as we uncover the tools and approaches to make our journey harmonious and anxiety-free.

Physical Symptoms of Anxiety: Heart Racing, Tail Tucks, and More

Just like humans, my anxiety also manifests in physical symptoms. When my heart races, it's not only because of my excitement to see you but also because of the adrenaline coursing through my veins in moments of distress. <u>You might feel the quickened beat against your hand as you place it gently on my chest.</u>

Another physical indicator is my tail. When anxiety takes hold, you may notice my tail tucked tightly between my hind legs. This is a clear sign of my discomfort and vulnerability. In contrast, a relaxed and wagging tail signifies contentment and joy. <u>Observing the position and movement of my tail can give you valuable insights into my emotional state.</u>

Pacing and restlessness are common manifestations of my anxiety. You might notice me wandering aimlessly, unable to find comfort or settle down. <u>This restlessness results

A Must Have Guidebook for Dog Lovers

from my heightened alertness and the overwhelming urge to find relief from the unease that consumes me.

One physical symptom that may concern you, dear owner, is my increased panting. Panting serves as a way to regulate my body temperature but can also be a response to anxiety. Rapid and excessive panting can indicate my emotional distress, so offering me a calm and soothing environment is vital to help me regain my composure.

As we navigate the intricacies of my anxiety, don't forget to pay attention to changes in my eating and drinking habits. Anxiety can affect my appetite, causing me to eat less or lose interest in food altogether. Conversely, some dogs may seek comfort in excessive eating or drinking as a coping mechanism. Monitoring my eating patterns can provide valuable insights into the severity of my anxiety.

Dear owner, by familiarizing yourself with my anxiety's non-verbal cues and physical symptoms, you become my trusted ally in the journey towards a calmer and more peaceful existence. Your attentiveness and understanding are the keys to helping me navigate the overwhelming world of anxiety. So, to continue our fascinating exploration of the language of anxiety, I've made a handy table in chapter 17 about me and my friends' anxiety signs. Please check out **"40 Popular breeds anxiety type, level, and Signs"**

Explore the Dark Side of Dogs Life

28   **Decoding the Language of Anxiety**

A Must Have Guidebook for Dog Lovers

Chapter 3

Digging into the Root Causes

Woof woof! Welcome to the captivating third chapter of our paw-some journey, where I, your loyal and affectionate furry companion, will dig deep into the root causes of dog anxiety. Join me as we explore the triggers that can send my tail wagging with worry, including separation anxiety, noise phobias, and social anxiety.

Separation Anxiety: Please Don't Leave Me Alone!

Oh, dear owner, the mere thought of being separated from you fills my heart with anxiety. Separation anxiety is a common and worse challenge for us dogs, born out of the deep bond and attachment we share with our beloved human companions. The fear of being left alone can be overwhelming, causing distress and triggering various behaviors. But fear not, for we can work together to alleviate this anxiety and create a sense of calm during our moments apart.

You might notice subtle signs of my growing unease when you begin preparing to leave. I may start pacing back and forth, panting anxiously, or even resort to destructive behaviors like chewing on furniture or scratching at doors. Please remember, these actions are not intended to be mischievous; they're a desperate plea for your presence and reassurance. So, let's explore some techniques to help me cope with separation anxiety and find solace in your temporary absence.

One effective strategy is to gradually acclimate me to your departures. Start by practicing short periods apart, gradually increasing the duration as I become more comfortable. This method, known as desensitization, allows me to adjust to the idea of being alone while building trust in your return. Remember to reward me with treats, praise, and affection for calm behavior during these practice sessions, reinforcing positive associations with alone time.

Explore the Dark Side of Dogs Life

Digging into the Root Causes

Engaging in toys or puzzles can also significantly divert my attention and keep me occupied while you're away. Please provide me with interactive toys that dispense treats or engage my problem-solving skills. Not only will these toys keep me mentally stimulated, but they will also provide a positive distraction from the anxiety of your absence.

Leaving behind a familiar item that carries your scent, such as a blanket or an unwashed piece of clothing, can provide great comfort in your absence. Your scent is a soothing reminder of your presence and can help alleviate my separation anxiety. Additionally, consider playing calming music or leaving on a white noise machine to create a relaxing environment while you're gone.

Implementing a consistent routine is crucial in alleviating separation anxiety. I can develop a sense of security and stability by establishing a predictable schedule for feeding, exercise, and alone time. A structured routine helps me anticipate and understand the pattern of our daily activities, reducing anxiety about when you'll return. Remember to greet me calmly when you come home, reinforcing the idea that departures and reunions are a natural part of our routine.

In some cases, professional help may be beneficial. If my separation anxiety persists despite your best efforts, consider consulting a veterinarian or a certified animal behaviorist. They can assess my specific needs and provide tailored guidance and support to address my anxiety.

Dear owner, our journey to conquer separation anxiety requires patience, understanding, and a joint effort. By implementing these strategies and showering me with your love and reassurance, we can build confidence, resilience, and a sense of security even when we're physically apart.

In the next chapter, we will explore the realm of noise phobias and discover how we can tackle this anxiety together. So, let's continue our adventure, hand in paw, as we uncover more tools and techniques to help me lead a calmer and more relaxed life.

A Must Have Guidebook for Dog Lovers

Chapter 3

Noise Phobias: Fireworks, Thunderstorms, and More

Boom! Crash! Bang! These sudden and loud noises can send shivers down my spine and cause my anxiety to skyrocket. <u>Noise phobias are a common trigger for us dogs, and they can make me feel helpless and frightened.</u> The world can become scary for me, whether it's the booming fireworks on celebratory occasions or the rumbling thunderstorms. But together, we can conquer these fears and create a sense of tranquility amidst the cacophony.

During these noisy episodes, you may find me seeking refuge in small spaces or hiding under furniture. My trembling body, heavy panting, or frantic attempts to escape reflect my desperate search for safety. <u>It's crucial for you, dear owner, to provide a secure and calming environment during these times of distress, offering me the solace and reassurance I desperately seek.</u>

Creating a haven for me can make a world of difference. Designate a quiet, comfortable space where I can retreat when the noise overwhelms me. <u>It could be a cozy corner in a room or a specially designated area with a soft bed and familiar items like my favorite toys or blankets.</u> This safe space will serve as a refuge where I can find solace and feel protected from the overwhelming noise. <u>Dimming the lights and playing soft, soothing music can also create a calming atmosphere.</u> The gentle melodies and low lighting help create a serene ambiance that counteracts the anxiety-inducing noise. <u>Additionally, consider using sound therapy or white noise machines to help drown out the scary sounds.</u> These devices emit.

gentle, continuous sounds that can mask or minimize the impact of the noises that trigger my anxiety.

Calming pheromone sprays or diffusers, infused with synthetic versions of the pheromones that mother dogs release to comfort their puppies, can also provide a sense of comfort and relaxation. These products can help create a soothing environment and reduce anxiety levels during noise-filled moments. <u>Consulting with a veterinarian or a certified animal behaviorist can provide further guidance on the appropriate use of such products.</u>

Explore the Dark Side of Dogs Life

Dear owner, your presence and reassurance are the most potent antidotes to soothe my anxious soul during these noise-filled moments. <u>Your calm demeanor and a gentle touch can work wonders in helping me feel safe and secure.</u> Avoid reacting to the noise with fear or anxiety yourself, as dogs can pick up on human emotions. <u>Instead, project a sense of tranquility and demonstrate that there is nothing to fear.</u>

Gradual desensitization can also play a significant role in helping me overcome noise phobias. This technique involves exposing me to the triggering sounds in a controlled and gradual manner, starting at a low volume and slowly increasing it over time. By pairing the noise with positive experiences, such as treats, playtime, or praise, you can help me form new associations and reduce my anxiety response. <u>A professional trainer or behaviorist can guide you through desensitization to ensure its effectiveness and safety.</u>

Social Anxiety: Making Friends and Overcoming Fears

While I may be your social butterfly at home, venturing into the world outside can stir up a whirlwind of emotions for me. Social anxiety can make meeting new dogs or encountering unfamiliar people a nerve-wracking experience. <u>The fear of the unknown and the unpredictability of social interactions can leave me feeling vulnerable and apprehensive.</u> But together, we can build my confidence and overcome these fears.

When faced with social anxiety, you might notice me displaying avoidance behaviors such as cowering, hiding behind you, or even attempting to escape the situation. I might become tense, bark excessively, or show signs of aggression due to my anxiety. These behaviors are my way of communicating my discomfort and seeking safety.

To help me overcome social anxiety, gradual exposure to new environments, people, and other dogs is the key. <u>Start with controlled and positive introductions, allowing me to interact with calm, friendly individuals, and dogs.</u> Creating an environment that fosters positive experiences and builds my confidence is essential.

A Must Have Guidebook for Dog Lovers

Chapter 3 33

Offering praise, treats, and gentle encouragement during social interactions can reinforce positive experiences and help me associate them with feelings of safety and reward. Remember to be patient and allow me to set the pace for these interactions. <u>Pushing me too far or too quickly can exacerbate my anxiety, so respecting my boundaries and comfort level is important.</u>

Training plays a vital role in helping me navigate social situations. By teaching me basic obedience commands, such as <u>Sit</u>, <u>Stay</u>, <u>Wait</u>, and <u>Leave it</u>, you can provide me with a sense of structure and guidance. Positive reinforcement, such as treats and praise, helps me associate social interactions with positive outcomes and builds my confidence over time.

<u>In some cases, seeking the assistance of a professional dog trainer or behaviorist can be beneficial.</u> They can provide specialized guidance and develop a tailored training plan to address my specific social anxiety challenges. With their expertise and your dedication, we can work together to help me overcome my fears and form positive social connections.

Remember, dear owner, patience, and understanding are the pillars that will help me overcome my fears. Be my advocate and protect me from overwhelming situations when necessary. By providing a supportive and nurturing environment, you can help me develop the confidence to face social interactions with ease and joy.

<u>Understanding the root causes of my anxiety is the first step in helping me overcome my fears and live a more balanced and joyful life.</u> Your unwavering support, patience, and love are the guiding light that will lead me through the darkest moments of anxiety. Together, we can conquer social anxiety and embrace a world full of new friendships and adventures.

Explore the Dark Side of Dogs Life

Digging into the Root Causes

Chapter 2 & 3 summary

Woof! I've got some exciting news for you, dear owners! In Chapter 17, you'll find an incredibly helpful table that's all about your furry friend's **anxiety signs** and **root causes**. It's like having a secret decoder for understanding your pup's worries! This table is designed especially for you, detailing the top 40 popular breeds and their unique anxiety indicators. It's a quick and easy reference guide to help you identify when your dog might feel a little stressed or anxious.

But wait, there's more! It's important to remember that while the table provides general signs, every dog is an individual with their own quirks and personalities. So, paying close attention to your dog's behavior and considering their unique experiences and background is essential. While the table is a fantastic starting point, reaching out to a professional is always a good idea if you have any concerns about your furry friend's anxiety. Your veterinarian or a knowledgeable dog behaviorist can provide personalized advice and guidance based on your dog's specific needs.

Being a loving and caring owner means being there for your dog when they need you the most. So, use the table in Chapter 17 as your trusty guide, but remember to listen closely to your dog's needs and seek professional help if needed. Together, we can create a safe and happy environment for our beloved furry companions! Check out "**40 popular breeds anxiety signs and root causes**"

A Must Have Guidebook for Dog Lovers

Chapter 4

Creating a Haven of Calm

Woof woof! Welcome to the cozy and tranquil fourth chapter of our delightful journey together, where I, your furry friend with boundless love, will guide you through the art of creating a haven of calm for me. This chapter will explore the essential elements of designing a calming environment, the power of positive reinforcement training, and the magic of consistency in soothing my anxious soul.

Designing a Calming Environment: My Safe Sanctuary

Oh, dear owner, a serene and soothing environment can work wonders for my anxious heart. As you seek solace in a peaceful setting, I crave a safe sanctuary that offers comfort and tranquility. Let's embark on a design journey as we create a haven of calm specifically tailored to my needs.

One of the key aspects of a calming environment is ensuring a designated space just for me. It can be a cozy corner in your home, adorned with soft blankets and pillows, where I can retreat when I need quiet time. Consider creating a den-like area with a crate or a comfortable bed, providing a sense of security and privacy.

Lighting plays a crucial role in setting the mood. Soft, diffused lighting can create a warm and inviting atmosphere, while harsh or bright lights can be overwhelming for my sensitive eyes. Experiment with different lighting options to find what brings the most tranquility to our shared space.

Calming scents like lavender or chamomile can create a serene ambiance. Use natural essential oils or specially formulated sprays to infuse the air with soothing aromas. These scents can help relax my mind and body, creating a peaceful environment.

Explore the Dark Side of Dogs Life

Creating a Haven of Calm

It's essential to minimize external stimuli that can trigger my anxiety. <u>Reduce loud noises by closing windows, using soundproof curtains, or playing calming music or white noise.</u> Limit exposure to external distractions that might heighten my stress levels, allowing me to unwind and find inner peace.

Dear owner, with your thoughtful efforts in creating a calming environment, you provide me with a sanctuary where I can find respite from the chaos of the outside world.

Positive Reinforcement Training: Paw-sitive Methods for Confidence

Oh, the joy of learning and growing together! Positive reinforcement training is a wag-tastic approach to boost my confidence and reduce anxiety. <u>By rewarding desired behaviors rather than punishing unwanted ones, we can build a bond of trust and cultivate a sense of security within us.</u>

Positive reinforcement training is based on rewards, such as treats, praise, or playtime, to reinforce behaviors you want to encourage. When I exhibit calm and relaxed behaviors, reward me with a tasty treat or lavish me with gentle praise. <u>These positive reinforcements help me associate calmness with positive experiences, reinforcing my confidence and reducing anxiety.</u>

Patience and consistency are essential when it comes to training. Break down tasks into small, achievable steps, and celebrate each success along the way. <u>As I gain confidence through our training sessions, my anxiety will gradually diminish, allowing me to face challenges with a wagging tail and a heart full of courage.</u>

Consistency is Key: Routines to Soothe My Anxious Soul

Consistency is key in helping me navigate the challenges of anxiety. Dogs thrive on routine and predictability, providing a sense of security and reducing uncertainty. By establishing consistent daily routines, you create a stable framework that allows me to feel safe and at ease.

<u>Set a regular schedule for feeding, exercise, and rest.</u> Consistency in these essential areas helps regulate my physical and mental well-being. Aim for consistent mealtimes, exercise sessions, and designated rest periods, giving me the structure to feel balanced and secure.

A Must Have Guidebook for Dog Lovers

Chapter 4

In addition to daily routines, consistency in training is equally important. <u>Use the same cues, commands, and reward systems during training sessions, ensuring I understand the expectations and respond appropriately.</u> Consistency in training methods and expectations helps me build confidence and reinforces positive behaviors.

Creating a consistent environment is also crucial in reducing my anxiety. <u>Minimize sudden changes or disruptions to my surroundings, as they can trigger stress and unease.</u> When possible, keep the layout of our living space consistent, avoid rearranging furniture frequently, and provide me with a designated area where I can retreat and feel safe.

Consistency extends beyond our immediate environment to our interactions and responses. <u>Be mindful of your behavior and emotional cues, as I can pick up on them.</u> Please respond to my anxieties with calmness, reassurance, and consistency. Your consistent responses help me understand that you are a reliable source of support and comfort.

Sleep is a vital component of my overall well-being.

<u>Like you, I need sufficient rest to recharge and maintain emotional balance.</u> Establish a cozy bedtime routine, ensuring a comfortable sleeping area and a calming pre-sleep ritual. <u>Consider providing a soft, supportive bed, dimming the lights, and offering gentle strokes or soothing music to lull me into a peaceful slumber.</u>

Remember, dear owner, that consistency requires patience and commitment. It is a journey that requires ongoing effort and adjustment. <u>Be flexible and adaptable, when necessary, but strive to maintain a consistent framework that fosters my emotional well-being.</u> Through the magic of consistency, you provide me with the stability and predictability I need to navigate the challenges of anxiety. <u>Your unwavering dedication and commitment are the foundation upon which my confidence and peace of mind will flourish.</u> Let us embrace the power of consistency and embark on this journey of healing and growth together. With your love and guidance, I can overcome my anxieties and lead a life filled with harmony and contentment.

Explore the Dark Side of Dogs Life

Creating a Haven of Calm

The predictable rhythm of our routine becomes the soothing melody that helps ease my anxieties and allows me to flourish. In this chapter, we have explored the art of creating a haven of calm for me. From designing a calming environment to implementing positive reinforcement training and embracing consistency, you have become a true expert in creating peace and tranquility in my world.

A Must Have Guidebook for Dog Lovers

Chapter 5

Paw-some Products to Ease My Anxiety

Oh, dear owner, in this delightful chapter, we dive into the world of paw-some products that can help ease my anxiety. From cozy comforts to engaging distractions, these magical tools can make a difference in soothing my worried heart. Join me as we explore the wonders of ThunderShirts, interactive toys, and other marvelous products that bring me comfort and relief.

Cozy Comfort:
Exploring the Wonders of ThunderShirts

Ah, the snug embrace of a ThunderShirt—a trustworthy source of comfort during stress and anxiety. ThunderShirts are specially designed garments that provide gentle, constant pressure to my body, akin to a warm and comforting hug. This gentle pressure has a calming effect on my nervous system, helping to alleviate anxiety and fear.

The beauty of ThunderShirts lies in their simplicity. These adjustable wraps fit snugly around my torso, providing a sense of security, and reducing the intensity of my anxiety symptoms. Whether during thunderstorms, fireworks, or other anxiety-inducing situations, the ThunderShirt wraps me in a cocoon of tranquility.

When fitting me with a ThunderShirt, ensure its snug but not too tight. The fabric should allow for unrestricted movement and breathing. Take time to introduce the ThunderShirt gradually, associating its presence with positive experiences. You can pair it with activities I enjoy, such as playtime or treats, to create a positive association. While ThunderShirts are a fantastic tool, they may not work for every dog. We have unique needs and preferences, so observe my reactions and consult with professionals if needed. Remember, dear owner, your attentiveness to my comfort is the key to our success.

Explore the Dark Side of Dogs Life

Engaging Distractions: Interactive Toys for Stress Relief

Playtime, oh, how it lifts my spirits and distracts me from the worries that plague my mind! Interactive toys are a woof-tastic way to engage my senses, redirect my anxious energy, and provide mental stimulation. Let's explore some of the paw-some options available to us.

Puzzle toys are a bark-tacular way to challenge my mind and keep me entertained. These toys often involve hiding treats or toys inside compartments, requiring me to use my problem-solving skills to discover hidden treasures. Not only do they provide a mental workout, but they also offer a rewarding experience as I uncover the hidden goodies.

Chew toys are paw-sitively delightful for me. Not only do they provide an outlet for my natural chewing instincts, but they also offer a soothing effect on my anxiety. Choose durable, safe, and appropriate chew toys specifically designed for dogs. They can help redirect my focus, alleviate stress, and promote healthy dental hygiene.

Calming toys, such as plush toys with soothing scents or heartbeat simulators, can work wonders in easing my anxiety. These toys mimic the comforting presence of a companion, offering a sense of security during times when you may be away. The soft textures and calming scents provide a source of solace, reducing my stress levels.

Remember to rotate and introduce new toys regularly to keep the playtime exciting and engaging. Interactive play sessions with you are also invaluable in strengthening our bond and providing a sense of security. Engage in games like fetch, hide-and-seek, or gentle tug-of-war to foster a sense of joy and alleviate my anxiety.

Woof! Let me tell you about some paw-some toys that I love to play with:

Plush Toys: These soft and cuddly toys make great companions for snuggling and carrying around. They provide comfort and can help ease anxiety or loneliness when my humans are away.

1. **Chew Toys:** Oh, how I love my chew toys! They're not just fun to chew on, but they also keep my teeth and gums healthy. Chewing on these toys helps to remove plaque and tartar buildup, preventing dental issues.

A Must Have Guidebook for Dog Lovers

Chapter 5

Rope Toys: Rope toys are paw-fect for games of tug-of-war with my humans or doggie friends. They provide an excellent outlet for my natural instinct to pull and tug, and it's a great way for us to bond while getting some exercise.

2. **Interactive Puzzle Toys:** These toys really get my brain working! I enjoy the challenge of solving puzzles to find hidden treats or rewards. It keeps me mentally stimulated and helps prevent boredom.

3. **Ball Toys:** Balls are classic and always a blast! Whether it's fetching, chasing, or just bouncing around, ball toys provide hours of fun and exercise. Plus, they help improve my coordination and keep me active.

4. **Squeaky Toys**: Squeaky toys are a blast! The squeaky sound they make when I squeeze them brings out my inner hunter. It's such a joy to hear that sound and it keeps me engaged and entertained.

5. **Tug Toys:** Tug toys are great for interactive play with my humans or other dogs. It's a friendly competition to see who's stronger, and it helps strengthen our bond and build trust. Plus, it's a good workout for my muscles!

6. **Food Dispensing Toys:** These toys are like a tasty treasure hunt! I have to figure out how to get the treats or kibble out, which keeps me mentally stimulated and prevents me from gobbling up my food too quickly.

7. **Frisbees:** I love catching frisbees in mid-air! It's a thrilling game that tests my agility and speed. Plus, it's a fun way to enjoy the outdoors with my humans.

8. **Dental Toys:** Dental toys are important for maintaining my dental health. They help clean my teeth, massage my gums, and freshen my breath. Chewing on these toys is not only enjoyable, but it also helps prevent dental problems.

Remember, every dog is unique, so choose toys that match your dog's size, age, and preferences. <u>Always supervise playtime and regularly inspect toys for any signs of damage.</u> And always enjoy playtime us!

Explore the Dark Side of Dogs Life

42 Paw-some Products to Ease My Anxiety

A Must Have Guidebook for Dog Lovers

Chapter 6

When Extra Help is Needed

Oh, dear owner, we explore seeking extra help in this chapter when my anxiety requires a little more support. While your love and care are invaluable, sometimes professional intervention and medications can play a crucial role in helping me find peace and balance. Let's dive into the realm of medications and professional support to embark on this journey together.

Medications: A Look into the Options

Medications may be considered part of a comprehensive treatment plan when my anxiety reaches a challenging level to manage through other means. It's essential to understand that medication should never be the first line of defense but rather a carefully considered option with guidance from a veterinarian or veterinary behaviorist.

Various types of medications may be prescribed to help reduce my anxiety. Selective serotonin reuptake inhibitors (SSRIs) are commonly used to regulate serotonin levels in my brain, promoting a sense of calm and stability. These medications work best when used in combination with behavioral therapy and training.

Another class of medications that may be considered are benzodiazepines, which have a sedative effect and can help alleviate acute anxiety. However, they are typically used for short-term relief due to their potential for dependency and side effects. Working closely with a veterinarian is crucial to determine the most suitable medication and dosage for my specific needs.

Remember, dear owner, medication should always be administered under the supervision of a veterinarian. Regular check-ups and close monitoring of my response to the medication are essential to ensure its effectiveness and make any necessary adjustments.

Explore the Dark Side of Dogs Life

When Extra Help is Needed

Seeking Professional Support: Behaviorists and Trainers

In addition to medications, professional support from behaviorists and trainers can be invaluable in helping me overcome my anxiety. These dedicated individuals have the knowledge and expertise to guide you and me toward emotional well-being.

A veterinary behaviorist is a specialized professional who can assess my anxiety triggers, develop a customized behavior modification plan, and provide guidance on training techniques. Their in-depth understanding of animal behavior and psychology allows them to address the root causes of my anxiety and develop a comprehensive treatment approach.

Working with a certified professional dog trainer can also be tremendously beneficial. They can help us implement positive reinforcement training techniques tailored to my specific needs. From desensitization and counterconditioning exercises to teaching relaxation cues, a skilled trainer can equip us with valuable tools to manage my anxiety and build my confidence.

You know what's amazing? There are special medications designed just for dogs like me! Here's some paw-some information about them:

1. **Flea and Tick Preventatives:** Ah, those pesky critters! Flea and tick preventatives are like magical shields that keep those little bugs away from my fur. They come in different forms like spot-on treatments or collars. By using them regularly, you can keep me itch-free and protected.

2. **Heartworm Preventatives:** Heartworms can be scary, but fear not! Heartworm preventatives are like superheroes that defend my heart. Whether it's chewable tablets or topical solutions, these special medicines ensure I'm safe from those sneaky heartworms.

3. **Pain Relievers:** Sometimes, just like you, I can feel a little achy or sore. That's where pain relievers come to the rescue! They help me feel better when I have boo-boos or achy joints. But remember, only give me pain relievers under the guidance of a veterinarian.

4. **Antibiotics:** When I'm not feeling well due to a bacterial infection, antibiotics are my heroes! They fight off those icky bacteria and help me bounce back to my usual energetic self. Always follow the vet's instructions when giving me antibiotics.

5. **Allergy Medications:** Achoo! Just like humans, I can have allergies too. It's no fun feeling itchy and uncomfortable, but allergy medications come to the rescue! They come in different forms like tablets or injections and help me feel better by relieving those bothersome allergy symptoms.

A Must Have Guidebook for Dog Lovers

Remember, <u>dog medications should always be administered under the guidance of a veterinarian.</u> They will provide you with the right instructions, dosage, and duration for each medication based on my specific needs.

Common Dog Diseases

Now let's talk about some common dog diseases. Don't worry, together we can face them head-on!

1. **Rabies:** Woof, this one is serious! let's dive into the world of <u>Rabies, a disease that every responsible dog owner should know about.</u> It's important to understand this serious condition and how it affects us dogs.

Reason: Rabies is caused by a virus that attacks the nervous system. It is commonly spread through the bite of an infected animal, such as raccoons, bats, skunks, or even other dogs. Once the virus enters our bodies, it travels through the nerves and can cause severe damage to our brains.

Signs and Physical Symptoms: In the early stages, it might be tough to spot the signs of Rabies, but as the disease progresses, some common symptoms may become noticeable. These include changes in behavior, such as increased aggression, restlessness, or anxiety. We may also have trouble swallowing, excessive drooling, and sensitivity to light and sound. You may notice that we become more withdrawn and prefer to hide in dark places.

Appetite Changes: Rabies can affect our appetite in different ways. Initially, we may experience a decrease in appetite, and as the disease worsens, we might refuse food and water altogether. This can lead to weight loss and dehydration, making it even more challenging for us to fight the virus.

Duration: The duration of Rabies varies depending on the individual dog and the progression of the disease. It can range from a few days to several weeks. Unfortunately, Rabies is almost always fatal once clinical signs appear. That's why prevention is key!

Medication: When it comes to Rabies, prevention is crucial. The most effective way to protect us from this deadly disease is through vaccination. Regular vaccinations administered by a veterinarian can ensure that we are shielded against Rabies. If you suspect that your dog has been exposed to a potentially rabid animal, <u>it's important to seek immediate veterinary attention.</u> However, once clinical signs of Rabies appear, there is no specific medication or cure available.

Explore the Dark Side of Dogs Life

When Extra Help is Needed

There's an excellent Animal Hospital I want to share with you, CVA Animal Hospital. Although it's located in the USA. Don't worry, you can still access valuable information from their website. They have a dedicated section on Rabies, which provides useful insights. You can use QR-code or find it at the following link:
https://vcahospitals.com/know-your-pet/rabies-in-dogs

Remember, it's not just about keeping us safe from Rabies; it's also about protecting the community and other animals. That's why many countries and states have strict laws and regulations regarding Rabies vaccinations. By keeping our vaccinations up to date, you're doing your part to prevent the spread of this dangerous disease.

Stay vigilant, my wonderful owner, and <u>never hesitate to reach out to our trusted veterinarian for guidance and support.</u> Together, we can keep Rabies at bay and ensure a healthy and happy life for both of us. Woof!

2. **Distemper:** Uh-oh, distemper is a yucky viral disease that can make me feel really sick. Let's sniff out some knowledge about Distemper, a highly contagious viral disease that can affect us dogs. It's important for you, as my caring owner, to be aware of this condition and its implications. Here's what you need to know.

Reason: Distemper is caused by a virus known as the Canine Distemper Virus (CDV). It spreads through direct contact with an infected dog or by exposure to respiratory secretions, such as coughing or sneezing. Puppies and dogs with a weak immune system are particularly susceptible to this nasty virus.

Signs and Physical Symptoms: Distemper can present a variety of signs, and the severity can vary from dog to dog. Some common symptoms include fever, coughing, sneezing, and nasal discharge. We may experience loss of appetite, listlessness, and eye and nose discharge that can become thick and pus-like. As the virus progresses, it can attack our nervous system, leading to seizures, muscle twitching, and even paralysis.

Appetite Changes: When infected with Distemper, our appetite often decreases. We may lose interest in our favorite treats and meals. This can be a concern, as it can lead to weight loss and a weakened immune system. Keeping an eye on our eating habits and ensuring we stay hydrated is important during this time.

A Must Have Guidebook for Dog Lovers

Chapter 6

Duration: The duration of Distemper can vary, but it generally takes several weeks for the virus to run its course. However, recovery is not always guaranteed, as some dogs may not survive the infection due to its severe nature.

Medication: There is no specific antiviral medication available to treat Distemper. Supportive care is typically provided by veterinarians to manage the symptoms and provide relief. This may include fluids to prevent dehydration, medications to control secondary infections, and supportive therapies to alleviate discomfort.

Prevention is the best approach when it comes to Distemper. <u>Vaccination is essential to protect us from this dangerous virus.</u> Regular vaccinations, as recommended by our veterinarian, can help ensure that we develop immunity against Distemper. <u>It's also important to limit our exposure to potentially infected dogs</u> and practice good hygiene, such as regular handwashing and cleaning of our living areas.

If you notice any signs of Distemper or suspect that your furry friend may be infected, <u>it's crucial to seek immediate veterinary attention.</u> Early detection and prompt care can improve the chances of a positive outcome. Stay informed and keep our vaccinations up to date, my paw-some owner.

3.   **Parvovirus:** Oh no, this one sound scary! Parvovirus is a highly contagious virus that affects my tummy. It can cause severe diarrhea, vomiting, and dehydration, especially in young puppies. It's important to understand the ins and outs of this virus so we can stay healthy and protected. Let's dive in:

Reason: Parvovirus is caused by the canine parvovirus type 2 (CPV-2). It spreads through contact with infected dogs or their feces. It's a resilient virus that can survive in the environment for a long time, making it easy for us to catch if we're not careful.

Signs and Physical Symptoms: When infected with Parvovirus, we may experience a range of signs and symptoms. These can include severe vomiting, often followed by diarrhea that is often bloody. We may become extremely weak and lethargic, showing little interest in our usual activities or playtime. Additionally, we may lose our appetite and refuse to eat.

Appetite Changes: Parvovirus can greatly affect our appetite. We may have a reduced or complete loss of appetite due to the illness. It's crucial to monitor our food and water intake closely and seek immediate veterinary care if we're not eating or drinking as we should.

Duration: The duration of Parvovirus infection can vary from dog to dog. On average, it lasts for about a week, but it can extend beyond that in severe cases. It's important to remember that recovery may take longer as our bodies need time to heal from the damage caused by the virus.

Explore the Dark Side of Dogs Life

When Extra Help is Needed

Medication: Unfortunately, there is no specific medication available to directly treat Parvovirus. Treatment mainly focuses on managing the symptoms and providing supportive care. This includes administering intravenous fluids to combat dehydration caused by vomiting and diarrhea. Antibiotics may also be prescribed to prevent secondary bacterial infections that can further weaken our immune system.

It's important to note that prevention is the best defense against Parvovirus. Vaccination is key to protecting us from this dangerous virus. Puppies require a series of vaccinations starting at a young age, and regular booster shots are necessary throughout our lives to maintain immunity. Following the vaccination schedule recommended by our veterinarian is crucial to ensure our protection.

To prevent the spread of Parvovirus, it's essential to avoid contact with infected dogs and contaminated environments. Regular handwashing and proper hygiene practices can help reduce the risk of transmission. Keeping our living areas clean and disinfected also plays a significant role in preventing the virus from spreading.

Remember, if you suspect that your furry friend may have Parvovirus or notice any concerning symptoms, it's vital to seek immediate veterinary attention. Early detection and prompt treatment can make a big difference in our recovery.

4. **Lyme Disease:** Those tiny ticks can cause big problems! Lyme disease is a bacterial infection transmitted through tick bites. It can make me feel achy and cause other uncomfortable symptoms. **Reason:** Lyme Disease is caused by a bacteria called Borrelia burgdorferi, which is transmitted through the bite of infected ticks, such as the black-legged or deer tick. When these ticks latch onto our skin and feed on our blood, they can transmit the bacteria, leading to Lyme Disease.

Signs and Physical Symptoms: The signs and symptoms can vary from dog to dog. Some common signs include lameness or limping, which may shift from one leg to another. We may also experience joint pain and stiffness, which can make it difficult for us to move around. Other symptoms may include fever, lethargy, and loss of appetite. In some cases, we may develop a characteristic circular rash around the tick bite area, though this isn't always present.

Appetite Changes: Lyme Disease can affect our appetite. We may experience a decreased appetite or even a complete loss of interest in food. It's important for you to monitor our eating habits and consult with a veterinarian if you notice any significant changes in our appetite.

Duration: The duration of Lyme Disease can vary depending on the severity of the infection and the individual dog's response. With proper treatment, most dogs show improvement within a few days to a few weeks. However, in some cases, if the disease

A Must Have Guidebook for Dog Lovers

goes untreated or becomes chronic, the symptoms may persist for a longer period of time.

Medication: To treat Lyme Disease, our veterinarian may prescribe a course of antibiotics, such as doxycycline or amoxicillin. These medications are effective in fighting the bacteria causing the infection. The duration of treatment will depend on the severity of the disease and the veterinarian's recommendations. It's important to follow the prescribed medication schedule and complete the full course of treatment to ensure effective recovery.

Prevention is key when it comes to Lyme Disease. You can take several measures to protect us from tick bites, such as using tick preventive products <u>recommended by our veterinarian</u>, avoiding tick-infested areas, and checking us thoroughly for ticks after outdoor activities. Prompt removal of ticks is crucial, as it reduces the risk of transmission.

When Extra Help is Needed

Vaccinations

Now, let's wag our tails and dive into the world of vaccinations. They're super important for keeping us dogs healthy and protected. Check out these helpful details about vaccinations, straight from my furry perspective:

Core Vaccines: These are the essential shots that shield us from common and potentially dangerous diseases like rabies, distemper, parvovirus, and hepatitis. We usually get a series of shots when we're puppies, and then regular booster shots to maintain our immunity.

Non-Core Vaccines: These are recommended based on our lifestyle, where we live, and any specific risks we might face. For example, there are vaccines for things like canine influenza, kennel cough (Bordetella), and Lyme disease.

Vaccination Dog-edules: Puppies usually start their vaccination journey around 6-8 weeks old, and we'll get multiple doses until we're about 16-20 weeks old. But it doesn't stop there! We'll need regular booster shots throughout our lives to stay protected. <u>Your awesome veterinarian will provide you with a personalized schedule for me, so you'll know exactly when I need my shots.</u>

Regular Check-ups: Visiting the veterinarian for regular check-ups is like a spa day for us. It's important for them to keep an eye on my overall health and make sure my vaccinations are up to date. Plus, it's a great opportunity for you to discuss any concerns or questions you have about my well-being.

Remember, getting vaccinated not only keeps me safe but also helps protect other dogs in our community. It's a paw-sitive step towards a healthier doggy world!

You're doing an amazing job, my human friend, by taking care of my medications and vaccinations. <u>Always consult with the veterinarian for the best advice on medications and the right vaccination schedule tailored just for me.</u> Together, we'll conquer any health challenges that come our way, because you're the best owner I could ever ask for! Woof!

In this chapter, we have explored the role of medications and professional support in managing my anxiety. <u>It's crucial to approach these options carefully and consult the appropriate professionals.</u> Each step brings us closer to creating a harmonious and anxiety-free life for me.

A Must Have Guidebook for Dog Lovers

Chapter 7

Nurturing the Caregiver Within You

Dear owner, in this chapter, we focus on the most paw-some caregiver of all—you! Taking care of myself and my anxiety is a rewarding but challenging task. It's essential to prioritize your own well-being so that you can provide the best care and support for me. Let's explore self-care for dog owners, finding balance, and seeking support in this loving journey we share.

Dogs' Hygiene, what we should know

Woof! Let me share some friendly advice about grooming and how it relates to dog anxiety. Grooming is super crucial for keeping us pups healthy and feeling great. While grooming doesn't directly cause anxiety in dogs, certain breeds can sometimes feel a bit stressed or anxious during grooming. Here are a few things to consider when it comes to grooming and dog anxiety:

Sensitive Paws: Some dogs are more susceptible to touch and handling, making grooming sessions slightly uncomfortable. Our owners need to be gentle and patient during grooming to avoid triggering any anxiety.

Scary Noises: Grooming often involves strange tools that make loud noises, like clippers or dryers. These noises can startle or frighten us furry friends. Creating a calm and quiet grooming environment can help us relax and feel more at ease.

Making It Routine: We dogs love routine! Introducing grooming as a regular part of our schedule from a young age helps us become familiar with the process and reduces anxiety. Inconsistent or infrequent grooming can make us associate it with discomfort or fear.

Explore the Dark Side of Dogs Life

Nail & Ear, Handle with Care: Some grooming tasks, like nail trimming or ear cleaning, require gentle handling and restraint. If we feel handled too roughly or restrained too tightly, it can make us anxious. Positive reinforcement, like treats and praise, helps us associate grooming with positive experiences.

Breed-Specific Needs: Depending on our coat type, every dog breed has its own grooming requirements. Some of us need regular brushing and grooming to keep our fur looking fabulous. Neglecting these needs can lead to discomfort and potential health issues, making us anxious.

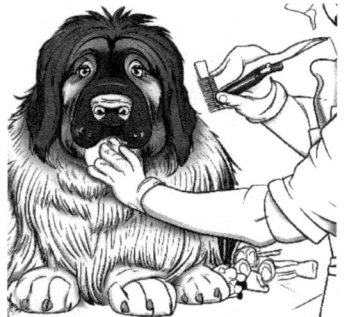

Grooming- anxiety-related tips:
Start grooming activities gradually with puppies so we can get used to it from an early age. Use positive reinforcement and rewards during grooming to make it a positive experience. If we get stressed or anxious during grooming, take breaks and resume when feeling calmer. Make sure to use grooming tools suitable for our specific needs and coat type. <u>If grooming becomes too challenging or overwhelming, consider seeking professional help.</u>

Every dog is unique, and our grooming needs and anxiety levels can vary. By being patient, understanding, and providing a positive grooming experience, you'll help alleviate our anxiety and make grooming time enjoyable for both of us. Woof!

Ok, fur-parents! Just wanted to let you in on a little secret: Chapter 17 is where you'll find a detailed and oh-so-useful table all about my friends, 40 popular breeds hygiene. It's like having a treasure trove of information right at your fingertips! This table covers everything you need to know about keeping your furry friend clean and healthy. From grooming tips to trimming, it's got you covered. Oh, BTW, always remember what I share is not enough. We are individually different! <u>You better always talk to a specialist, my friends' veterinarian.</u> So, head to Chapter 17 and get ready to unlock a world of dog hygiene knowledge. Please check out "**40 Popular Breeds Hygiene detail.**"

Self-Care for Dog Owners: Finding Balance and Support
<u>Caring for an anxious dog can be emotionally demanding, and nurturing yourself as you navigate this journey is essential.</u> Here are some paw-some self-care strategies to help you find balance and replenish your spirit:

A Must Have Guidebook for Dog Lovers

Chapter 7

✓ **Paw-sitive Practices:** <u>Engage in activities that bring you joy and relaxation.</u> Whether taking a leisurely stroll, practicing mindfulness, or indulging in a hobby, make time for activities that recharge your soul.

✓ **Connect with Nature:** Spending time in nature has a paw-some way of soothing the soul. <u>Take me for a hike or simply enjoy a peaceful moment in the park.</u> The beauty of nature can provide a sense of peace and rejuvenation.

✓ **Reach Out:** Don't hesitate to contact friends, family, or support groups who can lend a listening ear or provide a shoulder to lean on. <u>Sharing your experiences and feelings can provide comfort and a sense of understanding.</u>

✓ **Practice Mindfulness:** Mindfulness is all about being present at the moment, cultivating awareness, and accepting your emotions without judgment. <u>Incorporate mindfulness techniques into your daily routine to cultivate inner peace and resilience.</u>

✓ **Seek Professional Support:** <u>Just as I benefit from professional support, don't hesitate to seek guidance from therapists or support groups.</u> These professionals can provide a safe space to express your emotions and offer advice tailored to your needs.

Remember, dear owner, taking care of yourself is not selfish—it's essential. <u>By nurturing your well-being, you ensure you have the strength, patience, and love to provide the best care for me.</u>

54   **Nurturing the Caregiver Within You**

English Edition

 A Must Have Guidebook for Dog Lovers

Chapter 8

Finding Zen with Your Furry Friend

Hey there, my paw-some human! Are you ready to dive into the world of mindfulness with your fur-tastic companion? In this chapter, we'll wag our way into the art of mindfulness, creating a sense of calm and balance that will make our tails wag with joy. Let's embark on this zen-tastic journey together!

Embracing Mindfulness
What's the Woof All About? Let me break it down for you. Mindfulness is all about being in the present moment and finding inner peace. We'll discover how it can bring harmony to both of our lives, reducing stress and strengthening our bond. Get ready to unlock a whole new level of togetherness!

Mindfulness with Your Furry Friend
1.   **Pause and Observe:** Take a moment each day to pause and observe your furry friend. Notice their movements, their expressions, and their unique quirks. Be fully present with them without any distractions or judgments. Embrace the simplicity of just being together.

2.   **Deep Breathing:** Deep breathing is a powerful tool to calm the mind and body. Practice deep, slow breaths and invite your furry friend to join you. Feel the rise and fall of your bellies as you inhale and exhale together. This synchronicity creates a sense of connection and relaxation.

3.   **Mindful Walks:** Turn your regular walks into mindful adventures. Pay attention to the sights, sounds, and smells around you. Engage all your senses and encourage your furry friend to do the same. Let go of racing thoughts and enjoy the present moment as you explore the world together.

Explore the Dark Side of Dogs Life

Gentle Touch and Massage: Touch is a powerful way to bond and relax. Take moments throughout the day to give your furry friend gentle strokes or a soothing massage. Pay attention to their response and the sensations you feel as you connect through touch.

4. **Gratitude and Appreciation:** Cultivate an attitude of gratitude towards your furry friend. Take time to reflect on all the joy and love they bring into your life. Express your appreciation through words, cuddles, and treats. This practice fosters a positive mindset and deepens your bond.

Remember, dear human, mindfulness is a journey, and starting small is okay. The key is to bring awareness and presence to your interactions with your furry friend. Together, we can create a space of peace and serenity that nurtures both of our well-being.

In this chapter, we explore the world of mindfulness with your furry friend. We can find Zen together by embracing the present moment, practicing deep breathing, and engaging in mindful activities. Get ready to embark on a woof-tastic journey of togetherness and inner peace!

Mindful Moments

Paws, Breathe, and Let Go It's time to pause, take a deep breath, and let go of all the worries. I'll show you some simple techniques to practice mindfulness. From mindful breathing to grounding exercises, we'll stay present and connected, creating moments of tranquility.

1. **Set the Stage:** Find a calm and quiet space where you and your dog can relax without distractions. This could be a cozy corner of your home or a peaceful natural spot.

2. **Take a Deep Breath:** Start by taking a few deep breaths to center yourself and bring your focus to the present moment. Allow any tension or stress to melt away as you inhale and exhale slowly.

3. **Observe Your Dog:** Take a moment to observe your furry companion. Notice their body language, facial expressions, and the sounds they make. Pay attention to their movements and how they respond to their surroundings.

Chapter 8

Engage Your Senses: Engage your senses and encourage your dog to do the same. Notice the feel of their fur as you gently stroke them, listen to the sound of their breath or paws on the ground, and take in their unique scent. Allow yourself to be fully present in these sensory experiences.

4. **Embrace Silence:** Embrace moments of silence with your dog. Instead of filling the space with words, simply be with them in peaceful companionship. Dogs have a remarkable ability to sense your energy and presence, and this silent connection can be deeply meaningful.

5. **Practice Mindful Touch:** Take the time to give your dog gentle massages or cuddles. Feel the connection and love between you as you offer soothing touches. Pay attention to their reactions and respond to their cues, providing comfort and relaxation.

6. **Mindful Play:** Engage in playtime with your dog but do so mindfully. Focus on the present moment, fully immersing yourself in the joy of the play session. Notice the details of their play behaviors, the excitement in their eyes, and the sounds of their happy barks. Let go of distractions and be fully present in the shared experience.

7. **Express Gratitude:** During your mindful moments, express gratitude for your dog's presence in your life. Reflect on the joy and love they bring, and silently or verbally express your appreciation for their companionship and loyalty.

8. **Follow Their Lead:** Allow your dog to guide the pace and flow of your mindful moments. Observe their preferences and respond to their needs. Honoring their cues and interests will create a deeper connection and a more unified experience.

9. **Enjoy the Connection:** Embrace the deep connection and bond from these mindful moments with your dog. Treasure the peacefulness, love, and joy that arise during these shared experiences. Remember, it's not about the destination but the journey of being fully present with your beloved companion.

By practicing mindfulness with your dog, you'll cultivate a stronger connection, deepen your understanding, and create moments of pure joy and tranquility. Enjoy the mindfulness journey together and cherish the precious moments with your furry friend.

Explore the Dark Side of Dogs Life

Mindful Walks

Strolling in the Present Moment Picture this: we're going for a walk, but with a mindful twist. Let's tune in to nature, feel the ground beneath our paws, and notice the beauty around us. Our walks will become more than just exercise – they'll be opportunities for mindful exploration and bonding.

1. **Set the Intention:** Before starting your mindful walk, set an intention to be fully present and attentive. Leave distractions behind and enter the walk with a sense of curiosity and openness.

2. **Engage Your Senses:** As you walk, engage your senses fully. Notice the sensation of the ground beneath your feet or paws. Feel the warmth of the sun or the touch of the breeze on your skin. Listen to the sounds of nature around you, whether it's chirping birds, rustling leaves, or flowing water. Take in the scents of the environment and let them fill your senses.

3. **Stay Curious:** Approach your walk with a curious mindset. Observe the details of your surroundings—the colors, shapes, and textures. Notice the small wonders that often go unnoticed. Encourage your furry friend to explore and follow their lead, embracing their curiosity as well.

4. **Breathe Mindfully:** Throughout the walk, bring your attention to your breath. Take slow, deep breaths, and allow each inhale and exhale to anchor you in the present moment. Invite your furry friend to do the same, synchronizing your breath together.

5. **Gratitude Walk:** As you walk, practice gratitude by focusing on things you're grateful for at that moment. It could be the beauty of nature, the companionship of your furry friend, or any other positive aspect of your life. Express gratitude silently or out loud, allowing it to uplift your spirits.

6. **Mindful Movements:** Incorporate mindful movements into your walk. Notice the rhythm of your steps, the sway of your arms, and the way your furry friend moves beside you. Be aware of the sensations in your body and stay attuned to the present moment through movement.

Remember, dear human, a mindful walk is not about reaching a destination but about being fully present during the journey. Embrace the opportunity to connect with nature, yourself, and your furry friend. These moments of mindful exploration will deepen your bond and bring a sense of tranquility to your walk.

Creating a Zen Space
Making Your Home a Haven Home sweet home! We'll transform our living space into a haven of peace and serenity. Together, we'll create cozy corners, fill the air with calming scents, and surround ourselves with things that bring us joy. Our Zen den will be a place where we can relax and recharge.

Cozy Corners: Designate cozy corners in your home where you and your furry friend can unwind and find solace. Set up a comfortable bed or cushion, add soft blankets, and arrange pillows for extra coziness. Make it a dedicated space where you can both retreat and relax.

1. **Calming Scents:** Fill the air with soothing aromas that promote relaxation and create a peaceful atmosphere. Consider using essential oils in a diffuser or lightly scented candles, such as lavender or chamomile. Just ensure that the scents you choose are safe for your furry friend.

2. **Declutter and Simplify:** Create a clutter-free environment that promotes calmness. Keep your living space organized and free from unnecessary distractions. A tidy and simplified space can help reduce mental clutter and create a more peaceful atmosphere for both you and your furry friend.

3. **Nature Elements:** Bring elements of nature indoors to create a tranquil ambiance. Place indoor plants, such as peace lilies or spider plants, to purify the air and add a touch of greenery. Decorate with natural materials like wood or stones to create a grounding and earthy vibe.

4. **Joyful Decor:** Surround yourself with items that bring joy and positive energy. Display photographs of cherished memories, incorporate artwork or objects that hold special meaning or choose decor in colors that evoke feelings of peace and happiness. These meaningful touches will uplift your spirits and create a harmonious atmosphere.

Mindful Training

Explore the Dark Side of Dogs Life

Finding Zen with Your Furry Friend

Nurturing Connection and Learning Training time can allow us to grow closer while learning new things. We'll communicate with patience, understanding, and love. Being fully present in our training sessions will deepen our connection and achieve paw-some results.

Set the Mood: Create a calm and focused environment before starting a training session. Minimize distractions and choose a quiet area where you can both concentrate. Dim the lights or play soft, soothing music to set a relaxed ambiance.

1. **Practice Patience:** Approach training sessions with patience and understanding. Remember that learning takes time and that each step forward is an achievement. Stay calm and composed and avoid getting frustrated or raising your voice. Positive reinforcement and rewards will be our guiding principles.

2. **Be Present:** During training, be fully present and attentive to your furry friend. Please give them your undivided attention and focus on their cues and responses. Respond accordingly, and tune in to their body language, vocalizations, and expressions. This mindful presence will deepen your connection and understanding.

3. **Positive Reinforcement:** Use positive reinforcement techniques to encourage and reward desired behaviors. Praise, treats, or playtime can be motivating rewards that reinforce the training process. Celebrate small victories and progress, and let your furry friend know how proud you are of their efforts.

4. **Bonding through Training:** Training sessions are not just about learning commands but also about strengthening the bond between you and your furry friend. Embrace the opportunity to connect, communicate, and build trust. Enjoy the learning journey together and let the training sessions be a joyful and enriching experience for both of you.

A Must Have Guidebook for Dog Lovers

Chapter 8

Dog Music

Let me finish this chapter with a real story.

Woof, a while back, my humans and I embarked on an adventure to a new place. Now, let me tell you, the car ride was a bit ruff for me – all that rumbling and unfamiliar scenery. After a few hours, we arrived at a new house with new faces and a new room I've never sniffed before.

You know what happened next? Yup, anxiety kicked in. I was pacing like a champ, making sure every corner of the room was up to my safety standards. After a few hours we went to sleep. But then, my amazing human mom, she's like my guardian angel, pulled out her magic device and played some music from this place called YouTube. Can you believe it? Music from a tiny glowing box!

I was puzzled at first, gave her mobile phone a good sniff, and boom, something happened. The tunes captured my attention, and before I knew it, I was feeling... relaxed. Yeah, you heard that right! I felt the tension melt away, and I dozed off into dreamland faster than a squirrel darts up a tree.

I'm no expert in human gadgets, but I can tell you this: there are many ways to help us pups find our inner Zen. And that music? Oh yeah, I've got the link right here in case it tickles your ears too. Maybe it'll work wonders for your furry friends at home or hey, you can explore other soothing tunes. Scan QR code or use below link

https://www.youtube.com/watch?v=E2Gnu9JGro0

If copying the link seems like a ruff challenge, just give **YouTube** a quick visit and look up "Relaxing Music for Dogs (12 Hours of Dog Calming Music)". You'll sniff it out in no time. Let the calming tunes work their magic, my fellow furballs! I'm paw-sitive the link will still be there when you dive into my book. But hey, if it's taken a walk, don't worry! Just search for similar doggy tunes and let the soothing vibes do their thing.

Remember, sometimes it's the simple things that work like a charm. Stay chill and keep those tails wagging!

Explore the Dark Side of Dogs Life

Finding Zen with Your Furry Friend

A Must Have Guidebook for Dog Lovers

Chapter 9

Training, tips, and tricks

Hey there, my paw-some human friend! Are you ready to discover some dog training magic? In this chapter, I'm gonna let you in on a little secret that'll have your tail wagging with excitement. Get ready to sniff out the most paw-some dog training academies in town!

Different breeds' training characteristics

When training us dogs, there are some paw-sitively important things for our wonderful owners to keep in mind:

1. **Patience:** We're eager to learn, but it takes time for us to understand and follow commands. So please, be patient with us! We'll get there with your love and support.

2. **Consistency:** We thrive on routine and clear expectations. You need to establish consistent rules and use the same commands and cues every time. This way, we can understand what you want from us and feel secure in our training.

3. **Positive Reinforcement:** We absolutely love being praised and rewarded! When we do something right, please shower us with treats, praise, and belly rubs. This positive reinforcement encourages us to repeat good behavior and makes training so much more enjoyable.

4. **Timing:** Timing is everything in our training. When we perform a desired behavior, make sure to reward us immediately. This helps us understand which action led to the reward and strengthens the connection.

Explore the Dark Side of Dogs Life

Training, tips, and tricks

5. **Short and Engaging Sessions:** Our attention spans can be as short as a squirrel's visit to the backyard! So, keep our training sessions short and engaging. Short bursts of 5-10 minutes throughout the day work wonders. We'll stay focused and excited to learn!

6. **Distraction-Free Environment:** Initially, training us in a calm and quiet place with minimal distractions is best. Gradually introduce distractions to help us generalize our training in different settings as we progress. But please, no squirrels during training!

7. **Safety First:** Our safety is of utmost importance! Please use positive and gentle training methods. Never resort to physical punishment or scary techniques. And always ensure the training area is safe and secure for us.

8. **Socialization:** We love making new friends, both furry and human! Early socialization is crucial for our development. Introduce us to different people, animals, and environments so we can grow up to be confident and friendly companions.

9. **Clear Communication:** We're experts at reading body language and tone of voice. Use clear and consistent commands, gestures, and a positive tone to communicate effectively with us. We're always ready to learn and please you!

10. **Enjoyment and Bonding:** Let's make training a joyful experience! Have fun with us, be enthusiastic, and celebrate every small achievement. Training is a time to bond and strengthen our incredible connection.

Remember, every dog is unique, and what works for one may not work for another. <u>If you're finding training challenging or need some guidance, consider contacting a certified dog trainer who uses positive reinforcement techniques.</u> Together, with love, patience, and consistency, we can achieve amazing things! Let's wag our tails and embark on this training adventure together!

A Must Have Guidebook for Dog Lovers

Chapter 9

Once again, each breed has its own special qualities and training needs, so you'll discover what makes them tail-waggingly awesome! From the loyal and intelligent German Shepherd to the playful and energetic Labrador Retriever, you'll find a variety of breeds to explore. Whether you're interested in the active Australian Shepherd, the clever Border Collie, or the gentle and loving Golden Retriever, chapter 14 covers you.

Discover how the Beagle's scenting abilities make them fantastic trackers or the Belgian Malinois's intelligence and drive make them excel in various training activities. Unleash the potential of the Bernese Mountain Dog's gentle nature or the Boxer's enthusiasm for learning.

Remember, each breed is unique, so take the time to understand their specific needs and tailor your training approach accordingly. You'll build an unbreakable bond with your furry friend with love, patience, and the right training techniques. Happy training, and may your journey be filled with wagging tails and endless joy!

I'm excited to share some paw-some information about popular dog breeds and their training characteristics. In chapter 17 of my book, you'll find a comprehensive list of 40 popular breeds and their unique training traits. Please check "**40 popular breeds training aspects table**"

Sniffing Out the Best

It's time to put on our detective hats and sniff out the top-notch dog training academies in your area. These places are like schools for us cool canines, where we can learn all sorts of amazing things. Get ready to uncover the hidden gems that will transform us into training superstars!

1. **Research and Recommendations:** Start your search by researching dog training academies in your area. Look for academies with a positive reputation and a track record of success. Seek recommendations from fellow

dog owners, your veterinarian, or local dog-related communities. Their firsthand experiences can provide valuable insights.

2. **Visit the Academies**: Once you have a list of potential training academies, schedule visits to get a feel for the environment and observe their training methods. Pay attention to the cleanliness and safety of the facility, as well as the demeanor of the trainers and staff. A welcoming and positive atmosphere is crucial for effective learning.

3. **Training Philosophy**: Inquire about the training philosophy and methods used by the academy. Look for academies that prioritize positive reinforcement and force-free techniques. Avoid academies that rely on punishment or harsh training methods, as these can harm our well-being and damage the bond between you and your furry friend.

4. **Trainer Qualifications:** Ask about the qualifications and certifications of the trainers at the academy. Look for trainers with formal education and certificates from reputable organizations, such as the Certification Council for Professional Dog Trainers (CCPDT). Qualified trainers are better equipped to understand our behavior and individual needs.

5. **Class Structure and Curriculum**: Inquire about the academy's class structure and curriculum. Look for academies that provide a variety of classes tailored to different levels of training and specific needs. Whether you're looking for basic obedience, advanced training, or specialized courses, choose an academy catering to your goals.

6. **Training Methods and Techniques:** Ask about the specific training methods and techniques used during classes. Positive reinforcement techniques, such as reward-based training, are highly effective and foster a positive learning

A Must Have Guidebook for Dog Lovers

experience. Avoid academies that use aversive or punishment-based methods, as they can harm our well-being and hinder our progress.

7. **Reviews and Testimonials:** Read online reviews and testimonials from previous clients of the academies you're considering. Their experiences can provide insights into the training programs' effectiveness, the trainers' expertise, and the client's overall satisfaction. Look for consistent positive feedback and success stories.

8. **Trial Classes or Consultations:** Some academies offer trial classes or consultations to give you a firsthand experience of their training methods. Take advantage of these opportunities to assess the academy's approach, observe the trainers in action, and see if it aligns with your goals and values. By carefully selecting a reputable and compassionate dog training academy, you can unleash your inner superhero and embark on a training adventure that will strengthen your bond with your furry friend. Get ready to soar to new heights of training excellence and have a tail-wagging good time along the way!

Wag-tastic Classes
From Puppy Basics to Advanced Paw-ficiency Once you've found your dream academy, it's time to dive into the wag-tastic classes they offer. From puppy basics to advanced paw-ficiency, these classes are tailor-made to enhance our training skills. We'll learn commands, tricks, and manners that will make us the talk of the dog park!

1. **Puppy Basics:** Start with the puppy basics class if you have a young pup. This class focuses on socialization, basic commands like sit and stay, and proper leash manners. It's the perfect foundation for our training journey.

2. **Obedience Training:** Obedience training classes are necessary for dogs of all ages. These classes teach essential commands such as sit, down, stay

Explore the Dark Side of Dogs Life

and recall. We'll learn to respond reliably to these commands, making us well-behaved companions in any situation.

3. **Advanced Training:** Once we've mastered the basics, we must level up with advanced training classes. These classes challenge us with more complex commands, advanced tricks, and off-leash control. We'll become paw-ficient in our training skills and impress everyone with our abilities.

4. **Canine Good Citizen (CGC) Prep:** The Canine Good Citizen program is designed to evaluate dogs' behavior and manners in various real-life situations. CGC prep classes focus on preparing us for the CGC test, a great accomplishment that can open doors to therapy work or other dog-related activities.

Canine Good Citizen

Scan QR code or search for "Canine good citizen" or use complete below link: https://www.akc.org

AKC is not-for-profit, founded in 1884. I love their first statement *"At the AKC, we believe that all dogs can be good dogs, and all owners can be great owners, all it takes is a little bit of training, lots of love, and of course, plenty of praise along the way."*

5. **Agility and Sports:** If we're looking for high-energy fun, agility, and sports classes are the way to go. We'll learn to navigate obstacle courses, jump hurdles, weave through poles, and more. These classes provide physical exercise and enhance our focus, coordination, and teamwork.

A Must Have Guidebook for Dog Lovers

Chapter 9

From Puppy Basics to Advanced Paw-ficiency Once you've found your dream academy, it's time to dive into the wag-tastic classes they offer. From puppy basics to advanced paw-ficiency, these classes are tailor-made to enhance our training skills. <u>We'll learn commands, tricks, and manners that will make us the talk of the dog park!</u>

Workshops and Seminars

Unleashing Your Inner Genius Hold onto your floppy ears cause the fun doesn't stop at classes! Dog training academies also offer mind-blowing workshops and seminars. We'll get the inside scoop on everything from obedience to agility and even some doggy sports. Our brains and bodies will be working together like a well-oiled machine!

1. **Obedience Refresher:** Stay sharp with obedience refresher workshops. These sessions reinforce our foundational obedience skills and allow us to fine-tune our training techniques. It's a great way to keep our training on point.

2. **Specialty Workshops:** Dog training academies often offer specialty workshops focusing on specific areas of training or behavior. From leash reactivity to separation anxiety, these workshops provide valuable insights and techniques for managing and addressing specific challenges.

3. **Canine Sports:** If we're interested in exploring dog sports like flyball, dock diving, or scent work, dog training academies offer workshops dedicated to these activities. We'll learn the rules, techniques, and strategies to excel in these sports and have a blast while doing it.

4. **Behavior Seminars:** Behavior seminars delve into the science of dog behavior, helping us understand the reasons behind our actions and reactions. These seminars provide valuable knowledge about behavior modification,

Explore the Dark Side of Dogs Life

problem-solving, and creating a harmonious relationship between us and our human companions.

Remember, my paw-some human friend, attending wag-tastic classes and participating in workshops and seminars at a dog training academy will enhance our training skills and provide mental stimulation physical exercise, and strengthen our bond. Get ready to have a tail-wagging good time while unleashing our inner genius!

Unleashing Your Inner Genius Hold onto your floppy ears cause the fun doesn't stop at classes! Dog training academies also offer mind-blowing workshops and seminars. We'll get the inside scoop on everything from obedience to agility and even some doggy sports. <u>Our brains and bodies will be working together like a well-oiled machine!</u>

Sources and Tools

Building Your Training Arsenal Let's not forget about the paw-some resources and tools available at these academies. From training guides to interactive toys, they've got everything you need to become a training master. We'll explore how these tools can help us overcome anxiety and make training a blast!

1. **Training Guides and Books:** Dog training academies often have a selection of training guides and books that cover a wide range of topics, from basic obedience to advanced training.

2. techniques. These resources provide valuable knowledge and step-by-step instructions to support our training journey.

3. **Treats and Rewards:** Treats and rewards are essential tools for positive reinforcement training. Dog training academies offer a variety of high-quality treats that are tasty and motivating for us. They also provide guidance on using treats effectively to reinforce desired behaviors.

4. **Training Clickers:** Clicker training is a popular method that uses a clicking sound to mark

Chapter 9

desired behaviors, followed by a reward. Dog training academies can provide clickers and teach us how to use them effectively for precise communication and timing during training sessions.

5.   **Interactive Toys:** Engaging our minds and bodies through interactive toys can be a fun and rewarding way to train. Dog training academies may recommend specific toys that provide mental stimulation and help us learn new skills while having a blast.

6.   **Training Equipment:** Depending on the type of training we're involved in, dog training academies may offer training equipment such as agility obstacles, long lines, and harnesses. These tools can enhance our training experience and help us master specific skills and activities.

Building Your Training Arsenal Let's not forget about the paw-some resources and tools available at these academies. From training guides to interactive toys, they've got everything you need to become a training master. <u>We'll explore how these tools can help us overcome anxiety and make training a blast!</u>

Unleashing Your Inner Superhero
The Transformation Begins Are you ready to unleash your inner superhero? With the help of these dog training academies, we'll become the best versions of ourselves. We'll gain confidence, learn new skills, and strengthen our bond. Get ready to shine like the true superstars we are!

So, my four-legged companion, it's time to enroll in a dog training academy and embark on an adventure that will transform us into training legends. Sniff out the academies in your area, dive into the classes, and let's become the training superheroes we were born to be! Together, we'll conquer challenges, build lifelong skills, and create a strong and joyful bond that will last a lifetime. Get ready to unleash your inner superhero and embark on an exciting training journey!

The Transformation Begins Are you ready to unleash your inner superhero? With the help of these dog training academies, we'll become the best versions

Explore the Dark Side of Dogs Life

of ourselves. <u>We'll gain confidence, learn new skills, and strengthen our bond.</u> Get ready to shine like the true superstars we are!

So, my four-legged companion, it's time to enroll in a dog training academy and embark on an adventure that will transform us into training legends. Sniff out the academies in your area, dive into the classes, and let's become the training superheroes we were born to be!

Training Examples

Hey there, human friend! Let's have a tail-wagging good time while learning and bonding together!

Sit Pretty: Teach me how to sit like a pro! Hold a tasty treat above my nose and gently move it backward as I try to reach it. As I follow the treat, my bottom will naturally lower into a sitting position. Once I'm sitting, praise me and give me the treat as a reward. Repeat this a few times until I've mastered the art of sitting pretty!

1. **Shake a Paw:** Let's show off our handshake skills! Start by holding a treat in your closed hand and offer it to me. When I paw at your hand to try and get the treat, say <u>Shake</u>, and open your hand to let me have it. Praise and give me lots of love when I shake a paw with you. We'll be the best handshakes in town!

2. **High Five:** Who doesn't love a high-five? Hold a treat in one hand and raise it slightly above my head. When I reach up with my paw to touch your hand, say <u>High five</u> and give me the treat. Let's celebrate our teamwork with a paw-some high-five!

A Must Have Guidebook for Dog Lovers

Chapter 9

3. **Stay and Wait:** This one is all about self-control. Start by asking me to sit or lie down. Once I'm in position, hold your hand up like a stop sign and say <u>Stay</u> or <u>Wait</u>. Take a step back, and if I stay in place, praise me, and offer a treat. Gradually increase the distance and duration of the stay. Patience is key, and I'll become a master at staying put!

4. **Recall:** Let's practice coming when called! Start in a secure area, call my name enthusiastically, and then run backward a few steps while encouraging me to chase you. When I catch up to you, reward me with treats and lots of praise. This game of chase will make coming when called super exciting and fun!

5. **Leave It:** Help me resist temptation with the <u>Leave it</u> command. Show me a treat in your closed hand and say, <u>Leave it</u>. When I stop trying to get the treat, please give me a different treat from your other hand and shower me with praise. Gradually increase the difficulty by using more enticing items, like toys or food, on the ground. With practice, I'll become a pro at leaving things alone!

Remember, human buddy, <u>training should always be positive, fun, and filled with rewards and love. Keep sessions short and sweet, and practice regularly to reinforce what we've learned.</u> Together, we'll master these training examples and create an unbreakable bond. Let's wag our tails and embark on this training adventure together!

Explore the Dark Side of Dogs Life

Training, tips, and tricks

A Must Have Guidebook for Dog Lovers

Chapter 10

General Health
& 40 popular breeds anxiety summary

Health, Age, Vaccination
Woof woof! Today, we're diving into the fascinating dog health and wellness world. It's essential to understand how different factors like health, age, energy level, vaccinations, and preventive care can affect our furry happiness and keep those anxiety paws at bay.

First things first, let's talk about health. <u>Just like you, us dogs need regular check-ups</u> and care to stay in tip-top shape. We might encounter some common health issues or have certain predispositions based on our breed. That's why you must watch for any signs of discomfort or unusual behavior and take us to the vet when needed. Remember, prevention is key!

Speaking of age, as we grow older, our needs change too. Puppies are bundles of energy and require lots of playtime and training, while senior dogs may need a little extra TLC and a more relaxed routine. By **TLC**, I mean Tender Loving Care. As dog's age, we might require a bit extra attention and affection to ensure our well-being. **TLC** includes things like providing us with a comfortable living environment, offering gentle exercise suitable for our age, monitoring any health changes, and adjusting our routine to accommodate our changing needs. It's all about showing us extra love,  care, and support as we enter our senior years. We appreciate your understanding and the extra TLC you give us! Adjusting our activities and providing proper nutrition for each life stage ensures we stay healthy and vibrant.

Energy level plays a big role in our well-being. Some breeds, like the Border Collie or Australian Shepherd, have abundant energy and need plenty of exercises and mental stimulation to stay happy. Others, like the Bulldog or Shih Tzu, are more laid-back and prefer snuggles and leisurely walks. Matching our energy levels with the right amount of activity is essential for a balanced and anxiety-free life.

Explore the Dark Side of Dogs Life

General Health

Now let's talk vaccinations! Vaccinations are like superhero shields that protect us from harmful diseases. Each breed might have different vaccination requirements, <u>so it's important to follow your veterinarian's recommendations and keep our immunizations up to date.</u> This helps keep us healthy and prevents the stress of falling ill.

Preventive care is another crucial aspect of our well-being. Regular grooming, dental care, and parasite prevention keep us looking and feeling our best. It's like a spa day for us! Plus, proper nutrition and a balanced diet are essential to support our overall health.

But wait, there's more! In Chapter 17, you'll find a treasure trove of information in the form of a super useful table. It's like a goldmine of knowledge about 40 popular breeds and their specific health concerns, energy levels, vaccination periods, and preventive care needs. It's a quick and handy reference guide to help you understand and address potential health issues, and anxiety triggers for your specific breed. Please check out **"40 popular breeds General Health and age data"**

My Food

Woof, my furry friends! Let's have a break before I give a summary of my other breeds' friends. I want to talk about one of our favorite things in the world: food! As a wise dog, I want to guide you on what we can and can't eat to keep our tummies happy and healthy. When our tummy is full, we are cool... So, listen up, and let's dig in!

First things first, our food should be nutritious and balanced. We need a combination of proteins, carbohydrates, healthy fats, vitamins, and minerals. Our primary diet should consist of high-quality dog food that meets our specific nutritional needs. It's like a tailor-made menu just for us!

Now, here's a list of dog-friendly foods we can enjoy:
- Lean meats like chicken, turkey, and beef (cooked and boneless, of course!)
- Fish like salmon and tuna (cooked and free of bones)
- Fruits such as apples, bananas, and watermelon (in moderation and without seeds or pits)
- Veggies like carrots, green beans, and sweet potatoes (cooked and cut into bite-sized pieces)
- Whole grains like rice and oatmeal (cooked)
- Dairy products like plain yogurt (in moderation, as some dogs can be lactose intolerant)

A Must Have Guidebook for Dog Lovers

Chapter 10

But hold your leash! Not all foods are safe for us. Here are some things we should never munch on:

- Chocolate (a big no-no, as it can be toxic to us!)
- Grapes and raisins (they can cause kidney damage)
- Onions, garlic, and chives (they contain substances that are harmful to dogs)
- Avocado (the pit, skin, and flesh contain a substance called Persin, which can be toxic)
- Xylitol (a sweetener found in some human foods and chewing gum that is toxic to us)

Remember, our dear owners, this table is a great starting point, but treating us as individuals is important. Our needs might vary even within the same breed. So, keep a close eye on us, observe our behavior, and always consult with professionals like your veterinarian for personalized advice.

Oh, and speaking of food, let's have a serious chat about junk food. While those crispy potato chips or cheesy puffs may make your taste buds dance, they aren't good for us. Junk food can lead to weight gain, digestive problems, and even serious health issues. So, please resist the temptation to share your snack stash with us.

Remember, every dog is unique, so it's essential to consult with our superhero, the veterinarian, before changing our diet. They will guide you on your furry companion's specific dietary needs and portion sizes.

Lastly, let's be extra careful with our food storage and freshness. Keep our food in a cool, dry place, away from harmful pests. Check the expiration dates and make sure the packaging is intact. If you notice any changes in smell, texture, or appearance, it's better to play it safe and get a fresh bag.

So, my paw-some pals, let's keep our tummies happy and wagging by providing us with nutritious meals. With our loving owners' guidance and the vet's watchful eye, we can enjoy a lifetime of delicious and wholesome eating adventures. Bon appétit, my furry foodies!

Explore the Dark Side of Dogs Life

General Health

My checklist
Let's talk about something useful and practical, keep an eye out for these signs:

1. **Decreased appetite or eating habits**: It could be a sign of doggy blues if I'm not as excited about mealtime.

2. **Lack of enthusiasm or interest in activities:** Do you know how I usually jump around during playtime? Well, if I'm not as excited, something might be up.

3. **Changes in sleep patterns or excessive sleeping:** Dogs need their beauty rest, but it could be a red flag if I'm snoozing way more than usual.

4. **Low energy levels and reduced activity:** If I'm feeling blue, you might notice I'm not as active or playful as usual.

5. **Withdrawing from social interactions:** Normally, I love being around you and my furry friends, but if I'm avoiding social interactions, it's a sign something's not right.

6. **Behavioral changes such as restlessness or irritability:** If I'm acting differently, like being restless or irritable, it's my way of telling you I'm not feeling my best.

Now, what should you do if you spot these signs? Here are some follow-up actions:

1. **Observe and Document:** Keep track of any changes you notice in my behavior, appetite, or activity levels.

2. **Consult a veterinarian:** Make an appointment with a veterinarian to discuss my behavior and any concerns you have.

3. **Health Checkup:** The vet needs to give me a thorough physical examination to rule out any underlying health issues.

4. **Behavioral Assessment:** Consider seeking guidance from a professional dog behaviorist or trainer who can assess my emotional well-being.

5. **Environmental Enrichment:** Provide me with mental stimulation, interactive toys, and activities to help lift my spirits.

6. **Exercise and Play:** Engage in regular exercise and play sessions with me to promote my physical and mental well-being.

A Must Have Guidebook for Dog Lovers

Chapter 10

7. **Maintain a Routine:** Establish a consistent daily routine to provide stability and structure for me.

8. **Bonding and Affection:** Shower me with love, attention, and affection to strengthen our bond.

9. **Consider Therapy or Medication:** In severe cases, the vet might recommend therapy or medication to help manage my doggy blues.

Remember, every dog is unique, so the approach may vary. Just be attentive, patient, and compassionate with me. With your love and support, we can tackle dog depression together and positively impact my emotional well-being. Let's keep our tails wagging and our spirits high! Woof woof!

Explore the Dark Side of Dogs Life

40 Popular breeds anxiety summary

Now, I present a summary of my friends' anxiety levels. However, fret not! Each of them will take the stage later on, one by one, to share more details about themselves, along with adorable photos. You'll get the chance to delve into their unique personalities, quirks, and anxiety triggers. So, stay tuned and get ready to meet each of my wonderful friends up close and personal. Together, we'll unravel the intriguing world of dog anxiety and discover the best ways to support and understand our furry companions. Get ready for a tail-wagging adventure! Woof!

A Must Have Guidebook for Dog Lovers

Chapter 10

Alaskan Malamutes, known for their strength and endurance, are majestic and independent working dogs. While they are generally friendly and sociable, they can be prone to certain behavioral issues if not properly managed. Alaskan Malamutes may experience anxiety in situations such as separation from their human companions or changes in their environment. Signs of anxiety in Alaskan Malamutes may include excessive barking, howling, digging, or destructive behavior. To help alleviate their anxiety, their owners need to provide them with regular exercise and mental stimulation. Engaging them in activities such as hiking, sledding, or obedience training can help fulfill their physical and mental needs. Establishing a consistent routine and providing them with a secure and comfortable space can also help them feel more at ease. Positive reinforcement training techniques work well, as they respond positively to rewards and praise. Patience, understanding, and a loving approach are essential in helping them overcome their anxiety and thrive in a balanced and happy life.

Australian Cattle are intelligent and active herding dogs that may be prone to anxiety if not properly stimulated. They may exhibit anxiety through behaviors like excessive barking, digging, or hyperactivity. Providing them with regular physical exercise, mental stimulation, and a job to do can help alleviate their anxiety. These dogs excel in activities like agility, obedience, and herding trials, which can channel their energy and provide them with a sense of purpose. Structured training and positive reinforcement methods work best for Australian Cattle Dogs, as they respond well to consistent, reward-based training. With the right care, attention, and outlets for their energy, Australian Cattle Dogs can overcome anxiety and thrive as happy and well-balanced companions.

Explore the Dark Side of Dogs Life

40 popular breeds anxiety summary

Australian Shepherds, also known as **Aussies**, are highly intelligent and active dogs prone to anxiety if not properly managed. They may display anxiety through excessive barking, destructive chewing, or restlessness. Aussies thrive on mental and physical stimulation, so regular exercise, interactive toys, and training sessions is essential to help alleviate their anxiety. These dogs excel in activities like obedience, agility, and herding trials, giving them a sense of purpose, and helping channel their energy. Positive reinforcement training methods, consistent routines, and socialization are crucial for their well-being. With the proper care, attention, and outlets for intelligence and energy, Australian Shepherds can overcome anxiety and lead happy, fulfilled lives as loyal and loving companions.

Beagles, known for their adorable looks and friendly nature, may experience anxiety in certain situations. Signs of anxiety in Beagles can include excessive barking, howling, and restlessness. Their human companions must understand and address their anxiety to help them feel secure and at ease. Regular exercise is crucial for Beagles to burn off excess energy and maintain a healthy state of mind. Mental stimulation through puzzle toys and interactive games can help keep their minds engaged and alleviate anxiety. Creating a consistent daily routine and a calm and structured environment can give Beagles a sense of security. Positive reinforcement training methods work best for them, as they build confidence and reinforce good behavior. When Beagles feel anxious, gentle reassurance and comfort from their humans can make a big difference. With patience, understanding, and a loving approach, Beagles and their humans can work together to manage anxiety and ensure they lead happy and balanced lives.

A Must Have Guidebook for Dog Lovers

Chapter 10

Belgian Malinois, known for their intelligence and working ability, are highly active and driven dogs. While they are typically confident and focused, they can also be prone to anxiety in certain situations. Signs of anxiety in Belgian Malinois may include excessive barking, pacing, restlessness, or destructive behavior. To help alleviate their anxiety, their human companions need to provide them with regular exercise and mental stimulation. Engaging them in obedience training, agility, or scent work can help channel their energy and give them a sense of purpose. Socialization from an early age is crucial to help them feel more comfortable in various environments and around different people and animals. Positive reinforcement training methods work best for Belgian Malinois, as they respond well to rewards and praise. Creating a calm and structured environment, establishing a consistent routine, and providing them with a comfortable space to retreat to can also help reduce their anxiety. Belgian Malinois can thrive and lead a balanced and fulfilling life with proper care, training, and understanding.

Bernese Mountain Dogs with their gentle and affectionate nature, may experience anxiety in certain situations. Symptoms of anxiety in Bernese Mountain Dogs include excessive barking, pacing, and restlessness. Their human companions need to understand and address their anxiety to help them feel calm and secure. Regular exercise, particularly activities that engage their minds and bodies, is essential for Bernese Mountain Dogs to release pent-up energy and promote overall well-being. Providing them with a consistent routine, including feeding, exercise, and rest, can help alleviate anxiety and stabilize them. Gentle and positive training methods and socialization can build their confidence and help them navigate new experiences with less stress. Creating a peaceful and quiet environment at home, along with plenty of quality time and affection, can also help soothe their anxious tendencies. With proper care, patience, and understanding, Bernese Mountain Dogs can thrive and live harmoniously with their human companions.

Explore the Dark Side of Dogs Life

40 popular breeds anxiety summary

Bichon Frise, with their cheerful and friendly demeanor, may experience anxiety in certain situations. Signs of anxiety in Bichon Frise can include excessive barking, trembling, and clingy behavior. Their human companions need to understand and address their anxiety to help them feel secure and at ease. Regular exercise and mental stimulation through play and interactive toys are essential for Bichon Frise to expend energy and maintain a balanced mind. Creating a calm and predictable environment with a consistent routine can help alleviate their anxiety and provide them with a sense of stability. Positive reinforcement training methods and gentle reassurance and comfort work best for Bichon Frise to build confidence and reinforce good behavior. Providing them with a cozy and safe space where they can retreat when feeling overwhelmed can also help soothe their anxious tendencies. With love, patience, and a supportive environment, Bichon Frise can overcome their anxiety and lead happy and content lives alongside their human companions.

Border Collies, known for their intelligence and boundless energy, can be prone to anxiety if not properly managed. Signs of anxiety in Border Collies may include excessive barking, pacing, and destructive behavior. Their human companions need to provide them with plenty of physical exercises and mental stimulation to help them positively channel their energy. Regular training sessions and engaging activities like agility or herding can help satisfy their need for mental stimulation and provide a sense of purpose. Border Collies thrive in structured environments with clear boundaries and consistent routines. Socialization from an early age is crucial to prevent fear-based anxiety. Positive reinforcement training methods work best for Border Collies, as they are highly responsive to rewards and praise. Calming techniques, such as deep breathing exercises or puzzle toys, can help alleviate their anxiety and provide a sense of calm. With the right care, attention, and outlets for their intelligence, Border Collies can lead fulfilling lives and overcome any anxiety they may experience.

A Must Have Guidebook for Dog Lovers

Chapter 10

Boston Terriers are lively and affectionate dogs prone to anxiety if not properly managed. Signs of anxiety in Boston Terriers may include excessive barking, restlessness, and destructive behavior. Their human companions must create a calm and structured environment to help them feel secure. Regular exercise and mental stimulation through interactive play and puzzle toys can help alleviate their anxiety and burn off excess energy. Socialization from an early age is crucial to prevent fear-based anxiety. Positive reinforcement training methods work well for Boston Terriers, as they respond to rewards and praise. Providing them with a consistent daily routine and plenty of love and attention can help reduce their anxiety and ensure they lead happy and balanced lives. With the right care and support, Boston Terriers can overcome their anxiety and thrive as cherished companions.

Boxers are energetic and playful dogs prone to anxiety if not properly addressed. Signs of anxiety in Boxers may include excessive barking, pacing, and destructive behavior. Their human companions need to understand and address their anxiety to help them feel secure and at ease. Regular exercise and mental stimulation through interactive games and puzzle toys can help burn off excess energy and keep their minds engaged. Creating a consistent daily routine and a calm and structured environment can give them a sense of security. Positive reinforcement training methods and gentle reassurance and comfort can make a big difference in managing their anxiety. With patience, understanding, and a loving approach, Boxers can overcome their anxiety and lead happy and balanced lives.

40 popular breeds anxiety summary

Brittany, also known as Brittany Spaniel is a lively and versatile dog with a natural talent for hunting and retrieving. They are known for their intelligence, agility, and friendly nature. While they are generally well-rounded and adaptable, Brittany dogs can be prone to certain behavioral issues if their needs are not met. They may experience anxiety in situations such as being left alone for long periods or not receiving enough mental and physical stimulation. Signs of anxiety in Brittany may include excessive barking, restlessness, or destructive behavior. To help alleviate their anxiety, their owners need to provide them with regular exercise, mental stimulation, and social interaction. Engaging them in activities such as obedience training, agility, or retrieving games can help channel their energy and keep their minds engaged. Brittany thrive in environments where they receive ample attention, positive reinforcement, and consistent training. Creating a structured routine and providing them with a secure and loving environment can help them feel more secure and reduce their anxiety. With proper care, training, and a loving approach, Brittany can lead fulfilling and happy lives while forming strong bonds with their human companions.

Bulldogs are known for their friendly and laid-back nature but can also experience anxiety in certain situations. Signs of anxiety in Bulldogs may include excessive drooling, panting, or destructive behavior. Their human companions need to understand and address their anxiety to help them feel calm and secure. Providing a structured routine, plenty of exercises, and mental stimulation can help alleviate their anxiety. Bulldogs thrive on consistent training with positive reinforcement methods, which can build their confidence and help them cope with stressful situations. Creating a peaceful and comfortable environment with familiar and comforting objects can also help ease their anxiety. With patience, love, and a supportive approach, Bulldogs can overcome their anxiety and enjoy a balanced and contented life.

A Must Have Guidebook for Dog Lovers

Cane Corso is a powerful and majestic Italian breed known for its strength, loyalty, and protective nature. With a confident and stable temperament, they make excellent family companions and guardians. While generally a well-balanced breed, Cane Corso can be prone to certain behavioral issues if not properly trained and socialized. They may experience anxiety in situations such as being left alone for long periods or encountering unfamiliar people or animals. Signs of anxiety in Cane Corso can include excessive barking, restlessness, or aggression. To help alleviate their anxiety, it is crucial to provide them with early socialization, positive reinforcement training, and plenty of mental and physical exercise. Regular walks, interactive play sessions, and mental stimulation activities can help channel their energy and keep them mentally engaged. Establishing a consistent routine, providing them with a secure and structured environment, and giving them plenty of attention and affection is essential for their well-being. Cane Corso thrive in homes where they are treated as valued family members and receive proper guidance and leadership. With the right care and training, Cane Corso can be loyal, loving, and well-adjusted companions.

Cardigan Welsh Corgi is a charming and intelligent breed known for its distinctive appearance and spirited personality. With their short legs and long bodies, they have an adorable and unique look that captures the hearts of many dog lovers. Cardigans are highly adaptable and make great companions for both individuals and families. They are known for their loyalty, affectionate nature, and playful demeanor. However, like any breed, they may experience certain behavioral challenges if not properly trained and socialized. Cardigan Welsh Corgis may exhibit anxiety in various situations, such as separation anxiety when left alone or fearfulness towards unfamiliar people or environments. Signs of anxiety can include excessive barking, restlessness, or destructive behavior. To help manage their anxiety, it is important to provide them with early socialization, positive reinforcement training, and mental stimulation. Regular exercise and engaging activities like puzzle toys or interactive games can help them burn off energy and stimulate their minds. Establishing a consistent routine, creating a calm and structured environment, and offering reassurance and comfort are essential for their well-being. With proper care, training, and a loving environment, Cardigan Welsh Corgis can thrive and bring joy and companionship to their families.

Explore the Dark Side of Dogs Life

40 popular breeds anxiety summary

Cavalier King Charles Spaniels are known for their gentle and affectionate nature, but they can also be prone to anxiety. Signs of anxiety in Cavaliers may include excessive barking, trembling, or withdrawal. Their human companions must provide them with a safe and nurturing environment to help alleviate their anxiety. Regular exercise and mental stimulation through interactive play and training can help burn off excess energy and keep their minds engaged. Cavaliers thrive on positive reinforcement training methods, which can boost their confidence and strengthen their bond with their humans. Creating a consistent daily routine and ensuring they receive love and attention can also help ease their anxiety. With patience, understanding, and a calm approach, Cavaliers can overcome their anxiety and live a happy and balanced life.

Chihuahua, known for their tiny size and big personality, can be prone to anxiety. They may exhibit signs of anxiety through excessive barking, trembling, or aggression. Their human companions need to understand and address their anxiety to help them feel safe and secure. Regular exercises like short walks or interactive play sessions can help burn off their energy and reduce anxiety. Providing them a calm, structured environment and a consistent daily routine can also help alleviate their anxiety. Positive reinforcement training methods work well with Chihuahuas, as they respond positively to praise and rewards. Socialization from an early age can help them feel more comfortable and confident in different situations. With patience, understanding, and a loving approach, Chihuahuas can overcome their anxiety and enjoy a happy and fulfilling life with their human companions.

A Must Have Guidebook for Dog Lovers

Chapter 10

Cocker (English / Spanish), known for their beautiful coats and cheerful personalities, can be prone to anxiety. They may exhibit signs of anxiety through excessive barking, destructive behavior, or clinginess. Their human companions need to understand and address their anxiety to help them feel calm and secure. Regular exercises like daily walks or playtime can help release their energy and reduce anxiety. Providing them with mental stimulation through interactive toys or puzzle games can also help keep their minds engaged and alleviate anxiety. Creating a consistent routine and providing a safe and comfortable environment can give Cocker Spaniels a sense of security. Positive reinforcement training methods, gentle reassurance, and comfort can build their confidence and help them overcome their anxiety. With patience, love, and proper care, Cocker Spaniels can lead happy and balanced lives, enjoying their time with their human companions.

Dachshunds, with their long bodies and spirited personalities, can be prone to anxiety. They may display signs of anxiety through excessive barking, digging, or even aggression. Their human companions need to understand and address their anxiety to help them feel safe and calm. Dachshunds thrive on regular exercise, so providing them with daily walks or playtime can help them burn off excess energy and reduce anxiety. Mental stimulation is also important for these intelligent dogs, and interactive toys or puzzle games can keep their minds engaged and alleviate anxiety. Establishing a consistent routine and creating a secure environment can help alleviate their anxiety. Positive reinforcement training methods work best for Dachshunds, as they respond well to praise and rewards. When feeling anxious, gentle reassurance and comfort from their human companions can provide them with the support they need. With the right care, attention, and love, Dachshunds can lead happy and balanced lives, bringing joy to their families.

Explore the Dark Side of Dogs Life

40 popular breeds anxiety summary

Doberman Pinschers, known for their loyalty and protective nature, can sometimes experience anxiety. Signs of anxiety in Dobermans may include excessive barking, destructive behavior, or even aggression. Their human companions must understand and address their anxiety to create a secure and harmonious environment for them. Regular exercise is essential for Dobermans to release pent-up energy and maintain their overall well-being. Mental stimulation through training, puzzle toys, or interactive games can help keep their minds engaged and alleviate anxiety. Dobermans thrive on structure and routine, so establishing a consistent daily schedule can give them a sense of security. Positive reinforcement training methods work well with Dobermans, as they respond positively to rewards and praise. When feeling anxious, gentle reassurance and calmness from their human companions can make a significant difference in helping them feel at ease. With proper care, training, and a loving approach, Doberman Pinschers can overcome their anxiety and flourish as confident and well-balanced companions.

Chapter 10

English Cocker is a delightful and energetic breed known for its friendly nature and cheerful disposition. With their soft, expressive eyes and silky coats, they have an irresistible charm that captures the hearts of many dog lovers. English Cockers are versatile and adaptable, making them great companions for individuals and families alike. They thrive on human companionship and love being part of family activities. This breed is known for its intelligence and eagerness to please, making them relatively easy to train. However, they can be prone to separation anxiety if left alone for long periods. Signs of anxiety in English Cockers may include excessive barking, destructive behavior, or restlessness. To help manage their anxiety, it is important to provide them with plenty of mental and physical stimulation. Regular exercise, interactive toys, and engaging activities like obedience training or agility can help them burn off energy and keep their minds occupied. Establishing a consistent routine and providing a secure and structured environment can also help alleviate their anxiety. Positive reinforcement training methods work well with this breed, as they respond positively to praise and rewards. With love, patience, and proper care, English Cocker can thrive and bring joy and companionship to their families.

English Setters are known for their friendly and outgoing nature but can also experience anxiety in certain situations. Signs of anxiety in English Setters may include restlessness, excessive barking, or destructive behavior. Their human companions need to understand and address their anxiety to help them feel secure and comfortable. Regular exercise is crucial for English Setters to release their energy and maintain a balanced state of mind. Mental stimulation through training, interactive toys, or puzzle games can also help keep their minds engaged and alleviate anxiety. English Setters thrive on positive reinforcement training methods, as they respond well to rewards and praise. Creating a consistent daily routine and a calm and structured environment can give them a sense of security. When feeling anxious, gentle reassurance and comfort from their human companions can make a big difference. With patience, understanding, and a loving approach, English Setters can manage their anxiety and live a happy and fulfilling life.

Explore the Dark Side of Dogs Life

40 popular breeds anxiety summary

German Shepherds are intelligent and loyal dogs but can be prone to anxiety in certain situations. Signs of anxiety in German Shepherds may include excessive barking, pacing, or destructive behavior. Their human companions need to understand and address their anxiety to help them feel secure and calm. Regular exercise is crucial for German Shepherds to release energy and maintain mental well-being. Mental stimulation through training, interactive toys, and problem-solving activities can also help alleviate anxiety. German Shepherds respond well to positive reinforcement training methods, thriving on praise and rewards. Creating a structured routine and a safe and stimulating environment can give them a sense of security. When feeling anxious, gentle reassurance and comfort from their human companions can have a soothing effect. With patience, understanding, and consistent training, German Shepherds can manage their anxiety and lead a balanced and fulfilling life.

Golden Retrievers are friendly and affectionate dogs but can also experience anxiety in certain situations. Signs of anxiety in Golden Retrievers may include excessive barking, panting, or destructive behavior. Their human companions need to recognize and address their anxiety to help them feel safe and calm. Regular exercise is essential for Golden Retrievers to release energy and maintain a healthy state of mind. Mental stimulation through training, puzzle toys, and interactive games can also help alleviate anxiety. Establishing a consistent daily routine and a secure and stimulating environment can give them a sense of stability. Positive reinforcement training methods work well for Golden Retrievers, as they respond positively to rewards and encouragement. When feeling anxious, gentle reassurance and comfort from their human companions can make a significant difference. With patience, understanding, and a loving approach, Golden Retrievers can manage their anxiety and lead happy and balanced life.

A Must Have Guidebook for Dog Lovers

Chapter 10

Great Danes are gentle giants known for their calm and friendly nature but can also experience anxiety in certain situations. Signs of anxiety in Great Danes may include excessive drooling, panting, pacing, or destructive behavior. Their human companions need to recognize and address their anxiety to help them feel secure and at ease. Regular exercise is crucial for Great Danes to burn off excess energy and maintain a healthy state of mind. Creating a calm and structured environment and a consistent routine can give them a sense of stability. Positive reinforcement training methods work well for Great Danes, as they respond positively to rewards and encouragement. When feeling anxious, gentle reassurance and comfort from their human companions can make a big difference. With proper care, understanding, and a loving approach, Great Danes can manage their anxiety and live happy and balanced life.

Labrador Retrievers are friendly and outgoing dogs but can also experience anxiety in certain situations. Signs of anxiety in Labradors may include excessive chewing or digging, and they can be prone to separation anxiety, becoming destructive when left alone. To help alleviate their anxiety, providing them with plenty of exercises, mental stimulation, and interactive toys is crucial. Regular exercise helps them burn off excess energy and keep their minds engaged. Creating a consistent routine and providing a secure and calm environment can also help them feel more at ease. Positive reinforcement training methods work best for Labradors, as they respond well to rewards and encouragement. When they're feeling anxious, gentle reassurance and comfort from their human companions can make a big difference. Labradors can manage their anxiety and lead a balanced and happy life with understanding, patience, and a loving approach.

Explore the Dark Side of Dogs Life

40 popular breeds anxiety summary

Leonberger is a majestic and gentle giant known for its imposing size and friendly nature. With their thick, double coats and impressive appearance, they often turn heads wherever they go. Despite their large size, Leonbergers are known for their gentle and calm demeanor, making them excellent family companions. They are loyal and affectionate and enjoy being part of the family activities. This breed is highly intelligent and trainable, eager to please their owners. They are generally good with children and get along well with other pets when properly socialized. Leonbergers have a moderate energy level and benefit from daily exercise to stimulate them physically and mentally. Their coats require regular brushing to maintain their beautiful appearance and prevent matting. While they are generally healthy dogs, they may be prone to certain health issues, such as hip dysplasia and certain forms of cancer. Regular veterinary check-ups and a balanced diet are important for their overall well-being. With their loving and gentle nature, the Leonberger can make a wonderful companion for individuals or families looking for a loyal and devoted furry friend.

Maltese dogs are known for their small size and charming personality, but they can also experience anxiety in certain situations. Signs of anxiety in Maltese dogs may include excessive barking, trembling, or hiding. They are prone to separation anxiety and may become overly attached to their human companions. To help alleviate their anxiety, providing them with a calm and secure environment is essential. Creating a consistent daily routine, including regular exercise and mental stimulation, can help keep their minds engaged and reduce anxiety. Positive reinforcement training methods work well with Maltese, as they respond positively to rewards and praise. When they're feeling anxious, gentle reassurance and comfort from their human companions can help them feel more secure. With understanding, patience, and a loving approach, Maltese dogs can manage their anxiety and live happy and balanced life.

A Must Have Guidebook for Dog Lovers

Chapter 10

Miniature Schnauzer are delightful small-sized dogs known for their distinct appearance and spirited personality. While generally confident and outgoing, they can experience anxiety in certain situations. Signs of anxiety in Miniature Schnauzers may include excessive barking, restlessness, or destructive behavior. They can be prone to separation anxiety and may become overly attached to their human family members. To help alleviate their anxiety, providing them with plenty of physical exercises and mental stimulation is important. Interactive toys, puzzle games, and training sessions can help keep their minds engaged and reduce anxiety. Creating a calm and structured environment and a consistent daily routine can also give them a sense of security. Positive reinforcement training methods, such as rewarding good behavior, build their confidence and reduce anxiety. When they're feeling anxious, gentle reassurance and comforting gestures from their human companions can make a big difference. Miniature Schnauzers can manage their anxiety and lead a happy and balanced life with love, patience, and understanding.

Norwegian Elkhound is a beautiful and versatile breed with a rich history rooted in Norway. Known for its sturdy build and striking appearance, this breed is highly regarded as a loyal and courageous companion. Norwegian Elkhounds have a thick double coat that provides insulation in cold weather and gives them their distinctive look. They are renowned for their hunting skills, particularly in tracking and chasing games such as elk, bear, and other large animals. With their strong sense of smell and keen instincts, they excel in tasks requiring scent detection. Norwegian Elkhounds are also known for intelligence, independence, and strong-willed nature. They require consistent and firm yet gentle training to channel their energy and maintain good behavior. Socialization from a young age is essential to help them become well-rounded and adaptable dogs. This breed is typically friendly, affectionate, and protective of their families, making them excellent watchdogs. Norwegian Elkhounds are active dogs and need regular exercise to stimulate them physically and mentally. Their thick coats require regular grooming to prevent matting and keep them looking their best. Overall, the Norwegian Elkhound is a loyal, intelligent, and versatile breed that thrives in active households where they can receive the attention, exercise, and mental stimulation they need.

Explore the Dark Side of Dogs Life

Poodles are intelligent and elegant dogs known for their distinctive curly coats. Despite their sophisticated appearance, Poodles can experience anxiety in certain situations. Signs of anxiety in Poodles may include excessive barking, pacing, or seeking constant attention. They can be sensitive to changes in their environment and may require a calm and structured routine to feel secure. Regular physical and mental exercise are essential for Poodles to release excess energy and maintain their well-being. Engaging them in stimulating activities such as puzzle toys, obedience training, or agility exercises can help alleviate anxiety and keep their minds occupied. Positive reinforcement training methods, with rewards and praise, work best for Poodles, as they respond well to encouragement and gentle guidance. Creating a peaceful and quiet space within the home and providing comforting items like soft bedding or soothing music can help them feel more at ease. With the support of patient and understanding owners, Poodles can manage their anxiety and thrive in a loving and nurturing environment.

Portuguese Water is a charismatic and versatile breed with a fascinating history rooted in Portugal. Renowned for its robust physique and distinctive coat, this breed is highly regarded as an intelligent and affectionate companion. Portuguese Water Dogs have a hypoallergenic coat that is either wavy or curly, providing excellent water protection. They were originally bred for various tasks related to water work, such as retrieving nets, delivering messages between boats, and even herding fish into nets. With their natural swimming ability and desire to please, they excel in dock diving, water sports, and obedience training. Portuguese Water Dogs are known for their intelligence, trainability, and learning eagerness. They thrive on mental stimulation and require consistent and positive reinforcement training methods to keep them engaged and well-behaved. Early socialization is crucial to help them develop into well-rounded and friendly dogs. Portuguese Water Dogs form deep bonds with their families and are known for their loyalty and protective nature. They are generally good with children and can adapt well to family environments. However, they may be wary of strangers, so early socialization is essential to ensure they are comfortable in various social situations. This breed is energetic and requires regular exercise to stimulate them physically and mentally. Daily walks, interactive play sessions, and mental challenges are necessary to prevent boredom and keep overall well-being. The

Chapter 10

Portuguese Water Dog's unique coat requires regular grooming, brushing, and occasional professional trimming. With their intelligence, charm, and water-loving nature, Portuguese Water Dogs make fantastic companions for active individuals and families who can provide them with the attention, exercise, and mental stimulation they need to thrive.

Pug are charming and affectionate dogs known for their distinctive wrinkled face and curly tail. While they may be playful and outgoing, Pugs can also be prone to anxiety in certain situations. Signs of anxiety in Pugs can include excessive panting, pacing, or seeking constant reassurance. Their human companions need to understand and address their anxiety to help them feel calm and secure. Regular exercises, such as short walks or interactive playtime, can help Pugs release pent-up energy and promote a sense of well-being. Mental stimulation through puzzle toys or training exercises can also keep their minds engaged and reduce anxiety. Creating a consistent routine and providing a comfortable and safe environment can help alleviate their worries. Positive reinforcement training methods, using rewards and praise, are effective for Pugs as they respond well to gentle and encouraging approaches. Offering them a quiet and cozy space to relax, along with soothing scents or calming music, can help ease their anxiety. Pugs can overcome their anxiety and enjoy a happy and fulfilling life with love, patience, and a supportive environment.

Explore the Dark Side of Dogs Life

40 popular breeds anxiety summary

Rottweilers are powerful and loyal dogs known for their protective nature and strong guarding instincts. While they are often confident and self-assured, Rottweilers can also be susceptible to anxiety, manifesting in excessive barking, aggression, or destructive behavior. They can be prone to separation anxiety and may become overprotective of their family. To help reduce their anxiety, providing Rottweilers with early socialization with various people, animals, and environments is essential. Positive reinforcement training techniques focusing on reward-based methods can help build their confidence and reinforce desired behaviors. Mental and physical exercise are essential for Rottweilers to burn off excess energy and maintain a healthy state of mind. Engaging them in interactive games, obedience training, and challenging tasks can help stimulate their minds and alleviate anxiety. Creating a calm and structured environment with consistent routines can give Rottweilers a sense of security. With patient and understanding handling, along with proper training and socialization, Rottweilers can learn to manage their anxiety and thrive as well-balanced and confident companions.

Shiba Inu are small, spirited dogs known for their independent and confident nature. While they are generally a calm and reserved breed, Shiba Inu can be prone to anxiety in certain situations. Signs of anxiety in Shiba Inu may include excessive barking, destructive behavior, or withdrawal. To help manage their anxiety, providing them with a structured routine and consistent training is important. Positive reinforcement techniques work well with Shiba Inu, as they respond best to rewards and praise. Regular exercise and mental stimulation are crucial to keep their active minds engaged and to prevent boredom, which can contribute to anxiety. Creating a calm and secure environment, with a designated safe space for them to retreat to, can help alleviate their anxiety. Gentle reassurance and comfort from their human companions during stressful situations can also make a significant difference. With patient and understanding care, Shiba Inu can learn to overcome their anxiety and thrive as a well-adjusted and happy companion.

A Must Have Guidebook for Dog Lovers

Chapter 10

Shih Tzus are small, affectionate dogs known for their playful and outgoing personalities. While they are generally friendly and adaptable, Shih Tzus can be prone to anxiety in certain situations. Signs of anxiety in Shih Tzus may include excessive barking, trembling, or clingy behavior. To help manage their anxiety, providing them with a calm and structured environment is important. Creating a consistent daily routine and a designated safe space for them can help alleviate their anxiety and provide them with a sense of security. With rewards and gentle guidance, positive reinforcement training methods work best with Shih Tzus to build their confidence and reinforce good behavior. Regular exercise, both physical and mental, is crucial to help them burn off excess energy and keep their minds stimulated. Gentle reassurance and comfort from their human companions during stressful situations can also help calm their anxiety. Shih Tzus can learn to manage their anxiety and enjoy a happy and balanced life with a patient and loving care.

Siberian Huskies are energetic and social dogs known for their striking appearance and sled-pulling solid abilities. While they are generally friendly and outgoing, Siberian Huskies can be prone to certain behavioral challenges, including separation anxiety. When left alone for long periods, they may display signs of anxiety, such as excessive barking, destructive behavior, or attempts to escape. To help manage their anxiety, it is essential to provide them with regular exercise, as Huskies have high energy levels and require ample physical activity. Mental stimulation is equally important, as intelligent dogs thrive on engaging tasks and challenges. Building a consistent routine, including structured training sessions and interactive playtime, can help alleviate their anxiety and provide a sense of stability.

Additionally, crate training and creating a safe and comfortable den-like space can offer them a secure retreat. Positive reinforcement training techniques, such as rewarding good behavior and providing mental enrichment, effectively manage their anxiety. With proper care, attention, and a loving environment, Siberian Huskies can lead fulfilling lives and form strong bonds with their human companions.

Explore the Dark Side of Dogs Life

Staffordshire Bull Terriers, often referred to as Staffie, are friendly and affectionate dogs known for their muscular build and energetic nature. While generally social and good-natured, Staffie can be prone to certain behavioral challenges, including separation anxiety. When left alone for extended periods, they may exhibit signs of anxiety, such as excessive barking, destructive behavior, or attempts to escape. To help manage their anxiety, it is essential to provide them with regular exercise and mental stimulation. Daily walks, playtime, and interactive toys can help burn off excess energy and keep their minds engaged. Establishing a consistent routine and providing them with a safe and comfortable space can help alleviate their anxiety and give a sense of security. Positive reinforcement training methods, using rewards and praise, effectively teach them good behavior and build their confidence. With proper care, socialization, and a loving environment, Staffordshire Bull Terriers can thrive and form strong bonds with their human families.

Volpino Italiano is an enchanting and lively breed with a rich heritage originating from Italy. Known for its small size and fluffy coat, this breed captures hearts with its adorable appearance and charming personality. The Volpino Italiano has a thick double coat that comes in various colors, providing protection and adding to its delightful appearance. It is a companion dog through and through, forming strong bonds with its family and often displaying a loyal and affectionate nature. Despite its small stature, the Volpino Italiano is spirited and lively, always ready for play and adventure. This breed is known for its intelligence, agility, and quick learning ability. It enjoys mental stimulation and excels in activities such as obedience training, agility courses, and interactive games. Early socialization is important to ensure that Volpino Italiano grows up to be well-rounded and adaptable. Though small, they can be assertive and may show a protective instinct toward their loved ones. Regular exercise in the form of walks, play sessions, and mental challenges is essential to keep them physically and mentally stimulated. While their fluffy coats require regular brushing to prevent matting and maintain their beauty, they are considered a low-shedding breed, making them suitable for those with allergies. The Volpino Italiano is a delightful companion that brings joy and affection to its family. Their lively nature, intelligence, and captivating appearance make wonderful pets for individuals and families seeking a devoted and spirited canine companion.

Chapter 10

Welsh Springer Spaniel is a charming and versatile breed with a rich history rooted in Wales. With their distinctive coat and friendly nature, they capture the hearts of dog lovers worldwide. Welsh Springer Spaniels have a medium-sized, well-balanced build that enables them to excel in various activities. Their silky red and white coat is not only visually appealing but also provides protection against the elements. This breed is known for its exceptional hunting skills, particularly in flushing out game and retrieving. With their keen sense of smell and natural instincts, they thrive in tasks requiring scent detection. Welsh Springer Spaniels are intelligent and eager to please, making them highly trainable and responsive to positive reinforcement methods. They are versatile in their abilities and can participate in various dog sports such as obedience, agility, and tracking. Their friendly and affectionate nature makes them excellent companions and family dogs. They form strong bonds with their human family and are often good with children and other pets. Regular exercise is important to keep the Welsh Springer Spaniel physically and mentally stimulated. They enjoy activities such as brisk walks, jogging, and interactive play sessions. Their coat requires regular grooming to keep it clean and free from matting. With their loving temperament, intelligence, and energetic nature, the Welsh Springer Spaniel is ideal for active individuals or families looking for a loyal and devoted companion.

40 popular breeds anxiety summary

Yorkshire Terriers, or **Yorkies**, are small and spirited dogs known for their glamorous coats and confident personalities. Despite their small size, they can sometimes exhibit signs of anxiety. Yorkies may experience separation anxiety when left alone for extended periods, leading to behaviors like excessive barking, destructive chewing, or restlessness. To help manage their anxiety, their human companions need to create a safe and secure environment. Regular exercise and mental stimulation are essential to keep their minds and bodies active. Providing them with interactive toys and puzzle games can help alleviate anxiety and keep them engaged. Establishing a consistent daily routine and setting clear boundaries can also give them a sense of structure and security. Positive reinforcement training techniques, using rewards and praise, effectively teach them good behavior and boost their confidence. With love, patience, and a calm approach, Yorkshire Terriers can overcome their anxiety and thrive in a loving home environment.

A Must Have Guidebook for Dog Lovers

Chapter 11

Nap & Walk to stay tuned

Woof woof! First of all, I have some exciting news for you! In chapter 17 of our excellent book, I've added a comprehensive table all about napping and walking. It's a handy reference guide that will help you understand the specific nap and walk needs of 40 popular dog breeds. Isn't that paw-some?

Naps: Ah, the beauty of a good nap! Just like you, we dogs need our beauty sleep too. The amount of sleep we need can vary from breed to breed, but we like to snooze for about 12 to 14 hours a day. That may sound like a lot, but we must recharge our batteries and stay healthy and happy. So, please <u>provide us with cozy and comfortable spots to curl up and drift off to dreamland,</u> Zzz's**.** Please don't disturb us when we're having a blissful nap. It's our precious downtime!

In that table, you'll find important information about how many hours each breed typically needs to sleep and how much exercise they require through walks. You'll also discover whether these breeds are more suited to an indoor or outdoor lifestyle. This will better understand their unique needs and help you plan their daily routine accordingly.

Walks: Ah, the joy of going on a walk with our human companions! Walking is not just a physical activity for us; it's a chance to explore, bond, and engage our senses. The duration and intensity of our walks can vary depending on our breed, age, and energy levels. For some of us, a leisurely stroll around the block is enough, while others may need a more vigorous walk or even a run to burn off our excess energy.

<u>Regular walks are important for our physical and mental well-being, as they provide us with exercise, mental stimulation, and the opportunity to socialize with other dogs and humans.</u> So, grab that leash, put on your walking shoes, and let's embark on an adventure together!

But wait, there's more! The table also covers the exercise aspect, specifically walking. It reveals the recommended duration and frequency of walks for each breed, ensuring

Nap & Walk to stay tuned

we get the physical activity and mental stimulation we need to stay healthy and happy. Whether it's a leisurely stroll or an energetic hike, you'll have all the information you need to keep our tails wagging during our walks.

Remember, dear humans, it's important to consider our individual needs when it comes to napping and walking. Some breeds may require more or less sleep, and our exercise requirements can vary too. So, take the time to understand your furry friend's breed characteristics, consult with your veterinarian if needed, and create a routine that caters to our specific needs. And most importantly, enjoy these moments together! Napping and walking are not just daily rituals for us; they are opportunities for us to strengthen our bond, explore the world, and create cherished memories that will last a lifetime.

Lastly, the table helps you understand if a particular breed is better suited to an indoor or outdoor lifestyle. Some breeds thrive indoors, while others love to explore the great outdoors. Knowing this will help you create a living space that best meets our needs and keeps us comfortable and content.

So, my dear humans, flip to chapter 17 and dive into the wonderful world of napping and walking. Use the table as a valuable resource to understand your furry friend's specific needs, tailor their nap and walk routines accordingly, and provide them with a life filled with joy, rest, and adventure. Please check "**40 Popular breeds nap, walk and in/outdoor profile**"

A Must Have Guidebook for Dog Lovers

Chapter 12

Puppy Anxious World

My puppy time memory

Woof, my dear human friend! As I recall the days when I was just a tiny, fluffy puppy, it brought a mix of emotions to my furry heart. Those days were filled with joy and anxiety as I embarked on a new chapter of life away from my loving mother and littermates.

When the time came for me to leave my mom, I was filled with a mixture of excitement and fear. I was curious about the world that awaited me, but deep down, there was a sense of insecurity and uncertainty. Being separated from the comfort and warmth of my mother's presence was a daunting experience.

In those early days, I often felt anxious and overwhelmed. The unfamiliar surroundings, the absence of my mother's soothing presence, and the new faces around me intensified my worries. The world seemed big and intimidating, and I yearned for reassurance and a sense of belonging. But then, something extraordinary happened. My dear owners came into my life. Their warm and welcoming presence, gentle touch, and loving heart were like a beacon of light in those dark moments. They understood that I needed time to adjust and that my anxieties required patience and understanding.

They created a safe and comforting environment for me, filled with soft blankets, cozy beds, and toys that became my source of comfort. They showered me with love, attention, and gentle words that helped ease my fears. Their consistent routines and predictable schedules brought a sense of security that I desperately needed. During those dark days when my anxieties seemed overwhelming, they offered a listening ear and a comforting lap. They recognized my individual needs and worked with me, step by step, to overcome my fears. They gradually introduced me to new experiences, always respecting my pace and boundaries. But it wasn't just the dark days that defined our journey together.

There were also countless bright days filled with laughter, play, and an unbreakable bond. With their patient guidance and positive reinforcement, I learned to confidently embrace the world around me. Their love and unwavering support helped me grow into

Explore the Dark Side of Dogs Life

a confident and happy dog. We faced challenges and celebrated triumphs together, and our bond grew stronger through it all. They taught me that anything is possible with love, understanding, and a sprinkle of puppy treats. As I reminisce about my puppyhood, I'm grateful for the day they entered my life. They saw past my anxieties and believed in me. They provided a loving and nurturing home where I could flourish. Their warmth and care transformed my fears into courage, and I will be forever grateful for that.

So, my dear human friend, let us cherish every moment together, both the dark and bright days. Through it all, we will continue to navigate this beautiful journey of life, side by side, with wagging tails and hearts filled with boundless love.

A Must Have Guidebook for Dog Lovers

Chapter 12

From puppy to an adult dog stage

Woof! Now, let me take you on a journey through the different stages of a puppy's life, from my doggie perspective:

1. **Newborn Stage:** Ah, those were the days when I was just a tiny ball of fur, cuddled up close to my mama and siblings. I relied on her for everything - milk, warmth, and a sense of security. It was a cozy and safe time.

2. **Neonatal Stage:** As my eyes and ears started to open, I began to discover a whole new world around me. It was a bit overwhelming at first, but with each passing day, I grew more curious and eager to explore.

3. **Transitional Stage:** I wobbled on my little legs to keep up with my siblings. I started to develop my senses and learn about the different scents and sounds in my environment. It was an exciting time of growth and discovery.

4. **Socialization Stage:** This stage was incredibly important for me. I met many new people and furry friends and experienced different sights and sounds. It helped me become the friendly and sociable pup I am today.

5. **Weaning Stage:** Ah, the taste of solid food! It was a big step for me as I transitioned from relying solely on Mama's milk to exploring a variety of delicious treats. I discovered new flavors and textures, which made mealtime quite an adventure.

6. **Juvenile Stage:** Oh boy, this stage was full of energy and mischief! I had boundless curiosity and couldn't resist exploring everything in sight. I learned the basics of training, played lots of games, and discovered my unique personality.

7. **Adolescent Stage:** This stage had its ups and downs. I had bursts of independence and sometimes tested the boundaries. Hormones were buzzing, and I went through some changes. Thankfully, with patient guidance from my humans, I navigated this phase with love and support.

Explore the Dark Side of Dogs Life

8. **Young Adult Stage:** Ah, the stage of maturity! I settled into my adult self, both physically and mentally. I became more confident and experienced. Life became a balance of playfulness and responsibility.

9. **Adult Stage:** Now, I'm all grown up! I've reached my full potential and enjoyed the prime of my life. I still have lots of energy and love to give, but I also appreciate a good nap and a cozy relaxing spot.

Each stage brought its own set of adventures, challenges, and growth. And through it all, my humans were there, guiding, nurturing, and giving me all the love and care I needed to become the wonderful dog I am today. Woof! Please you do the same for your beloved puppy to adult stage.

New puppy, pup-to-human advice

Woof! So, you've decided to bring a puppy into your life. Well, let me give you some pup-to-human advice on what you should know to ensure a paw-some start for both of you. Here we go:

1. **Commitment:** Bringing home a puppy means committing to their well-being for many years to come. They need your time, attention, and love, so be prepared for a lifelong furry friendship.

2. **Puppy-proofing:** Puppies are curious little creatures who love to explore with their mouths. <u>Make sure to puppy-proof your home by removing any potential dangers or chewable temptations. Watch for electrical cords, toxic plants, and small objects that could be swallowed.</u>

3. **Socialization:** Early socialization is key to helping your pup become a confident and well-adjusted dog. Introduce them to new people, animals, and environments in a positive and controlled way. This will help them develop good manners and prevent anxiety in unfamiliar situations.

4. **Training and Discipline:** Start training your puppy from the moment they arrive. Teach them basic commands, housebreaking, and proper behavior using positive reinforcement. <u>Treats, praise, and consistency will work wonders. Remember, a gentle paw is much better than a harsh word.</u>

A Must Have Guidebook for Dog Lovers

5. **Health and Wellness:** Schedule a visit to the vet to ensure your puppy is healthy and up to date on vaccinations. Establish a regular feeding schedule with a nutritious diet suitable for their age and breed. Grooming, including brushing their coat and teeth, keeps them looking and feeling their best.

6. **Exercise and Stimulation:** Puppies have energy for days! Make sure to provide them with plenty of exercise and mental stimulation. Daily walks, playtime, and interactive toys or games will keep them happy and prevent them from becoming bored or mischievous.

7. **Patience and Love:** Your puppy is still learning and adjusting to their new surroundings**. Be patient with them** as they navigate their way through this big world. Show them lots of love, attention, and affection to build a strong bond based on trust and positive reinforcement.

8. **Puppy Care Resources:** There's a whole world of helpful puppy care resources out there. Books, websites, and local puppy training classes can provide you with valuable guidance on everything from basic care to behavior and training techniques. Seek out these resources to support you on your puppy parenting journey.

Keeping these points in mind and creating a loving and supportive environment will help your puppy grow into a happy and well-rounded dog. Enjoy every precious moment and cherish the paw-some memories you'll create together! Woof!

Puppy challenges and solutions

First things first, housebreaking can be a bit of a ruff challenge. Puppies need to learn where to do their business. Create a consistent routine for potty breaks, give lots of praise and treats when they go in the right spot, and be patient. Accidents happen, but they'll catch on with time and positive reinforcement.

Chewing and biting might make you go "ouch!" Puppies love exploring with their mouths, which means they may munch on your shoes or nip at your fingers. Give them plenty of chew toys and redirect their attention when they start gnawing at your favorite things. Teaching them to bite inhibition and rewarding gentle play will help them understand what's appropriate.

Explore the Dark Side of Dogs Life

Socialization is sometimes awkward! Introduce your puppy to new people, animals, and environments gradually and with many positive experiences. Puppy socialization classes are paw-some for meeting other furry friends and learning to be confident in new situations. It'll help them become well-rounded doggo!

Training takes time and treats. Be consistent and use positive reinforcement methods. Treats, praise, and rewards will help them understand what you want them to do. If you need extra help, puppy training classes are a paw-some option. They'll guide you and your pup on the right path.

Separation anxiety can be a howling challenge. Being separated from their littermates and mom can make them feel anxious. Start by leaving them alone for short periods and gradually increase the time. Create a cozy space for them, leave interactive toys to keep them busy, and try soothing music or pheromone diffusers to help them relax.

Teething can be a bit **ruff** too. Puppies love to chew when their teeth are growing. Please provide them with appropriate teething toys to soothe their gums. Keep valuable or dangerous items out of reach, and make sure to puppy-proof your home. We can't resist a good chew, you know!

Energy, energy, energy! Puppies have lots of it. They need daily exercise and mental stimulation to keep them happy and well-behaved. Take them for walks, play games, and give them puzzle toys to keep their minds sharp. A tired puppy is a good puppy!

Remember, patience and consistency are the keys to success. Raising a puppy takes time and effort, but the rewards are paw-some. Set clear boundaries, reward good behavior, and avoid harsh punishments. Seek professional guidance if needed, as they can give you personalized advice.

So, prepare for many snuggles, slobbery kisses, and endless tail wagging. Your new furry friend will bring so much joy to your life. Just remember, you're not alone in this journey. Contact other dog lovers, trainers, or veterinarians if you need a helping paw. Enjoy the puppy days and cherish every wagging moment. Woof woof!

A Must Have Guidebook for Dog Lovers

Chapter 12

Woof! I also have some exciting news to share about Chapter 17 of my book! In this chapter, I've added a special and incredibly useful table packed with valuable information that every puppy owner should know. You will find a detailed breakdown of your adorable pup's growth and development from week 1 to adulthood. Each table row represents a different age range, from those precious early weeks to the more mature stages of puppyhood. You'll discover key insights into your puppy's physical and behavioral development within the table. It's fascinating to see how their tiny bodies transform, and their personalities start to shine.

But that's not all! It covers essential aspects of puppy care, such as health care, feeding schedules, potty training, socialization, etc. It serves as a helpful roadmap to ensure you're providing the best possible care and support for your furry companion.

Remember, every puppy is unique and may progress at their own pace, but this table will give you a general overview of what to expect during each stage of your puppy's life. It's a valuable resource that can help you navigate through the joys and challenges of raising a puppy. <u>Always consult with your veterinarian for specific vaccination schedules and dietary recommendations tailored to your puppy's breed, size, and health requirements.</u>

So, make sure to flip to Chapter 17 and take a peek at the **"Puppy Life Stage Development Table"** Happy reading and enjoy watching your furry friend grow and thrive! Woof!

Explore the Dark Side of Dogs Life

Puppy Anxious World

A Must Have Guidebook for Dog Lovers

Chapter 13

Last But Not Least

Woof! We've made it to the end of our amazing adventure, my paw-some human pals. Together, we've dug deep into the mysterious world of dog anxiety, unraveled its secrets, and sniffed out ways to bring more joy and peace into our lives.

We've learned to speak the language of anxiety, reading each other's signals like a boss. We've got the inside scoop from the telltale signs we give off when we're anxious to the physical symptoms that make our tails tuck and our hearts race.

We've sniffed out the root causes, like separation anxiety when you leave us alone and noise phobias that turn us into quivering balls of fur during thunderstorms and fireworks. And let's not forget about social anxiety, where we learn to make friends and conquer our fears like the brave pups we are.

But don't worry my loyal humans, we've also discovered the secrets to creating a chill zone that's fit for a dog. We've learned how positive reinforcement training can boost our confidence and build a tighter bond than a tennis ball knot. And we've seen that consistency is key, with routines that bring us comfort and stability.

And oh boy, have we unleashed some tail-wagging products that make our anxiety take a backseat. From snug ThunderShirts that wrap us in a cozy embrace to interactive toys that keep us entertained and distracted, we've got the tools to conquer those worry moments.

Sometimes we might need some extra help, and that's where medications and professional support from behaviorists and trainers can save the day. They're like the superheroes of the doggy world, swooping in to lend a helping paw when we need it most.

But here's the scoop, my awesome humans: this journey isn't just about us. It's about you too! Take care of yourselves, find your balance, and don't hesitate to ask for support

Explore the Dark Side of Dogs Life

Last But Not Least

when needed. When you're at your best, you can give us the love and care that makes our tails wag like crazy.

Remember, this book serves as a guide—a steppingstone towards a happier, more balanced life. Each dog is unique, and it's essential to tailor the strategies and techniques to my individual needs. <u>Consult with professionals, adapt, and modify the suggestions to create a personalized plan that best supports my well-being.</u>

Do you remember the anxious face I had in the "Preface" when I first started writing this book? Well, now take a look at my happy face after you've read my words. Your understanding and commitment mean the world to me, and I have even more trust in you to always take care of me. Thank you for delving into the depths of dog anxiety and learning how to provide a calmer, happier life for me and my fellow furry friends. From the bottom of my heart, thank you for being the paw-some human companion I need and deserve.

Woof woof! I'm wagging my tail in anticipation and woofing with excitement as I invite you to share your feedback, heart-warming stories, and helpful notes with me. I'd love to hear from you and learn about your experiences with my book. So, grab that keyboard, type away, and send your woofs to my email address. Together, we can make a difference and create a paw-some community supporting dogs everywhere. Thank you for being a part of this tail-wagging adventure!

Don't hesitate to reach out if you have a success story to share, a question that's been bugging you, or just want to shower me with some belly rub love. Your woofs mean the world to me! Once again, please keep in touch to help my dog pals!

<u>worriestowags@gmail.com</u>

You can also find me in Instagram, please follow me at "**Worries to Wags**" for a wag-tastic experience filled with adorable pictures, paw-some adventures, and helpful tips for a happy and healthy life with your furry companions. Let's embark on this furry friendship together, where we can share our love for dog-related things. You'll find it all in one place, whether it's funny videos, heartwarming stories, or training tricks. Plus, you'll get sneak peeks into my daily adventures and behind-the-scenes of my upcoming projects. Scan QR Code, or search for "@Worries to Wag"; otherwise, here is the complete link:

@WORRIES_TO_WAGS

<u>https://instagram.com/worries_to_wags?igshid=OGQ5ZDc2ODk2ZA==</u>

A Must Have Guidebook for Dog Lovers

Chapter 13

So, grab your humans, tap that **Follow** button, and join the pack. Together, we'll create a community of dog lovers who celebrate the joy, companionship, and unconditional love our four-legged friends bring into our lives.

Dear human-pal, as we conclude this tail-wagging adventure, remember that our journey together is filled with boundless love, trust, and understanding. With your unwavering support, we can face our anxiety with courage and find solace in the warmth of our shared moments.

Hold your leash, there's more to explore! Flip those pages and uncover details about 40 popular breeds, my furry pals, and a treasure trove of info waiting for you.

On behalf of all my other breeds' pal, thank you for being the paw-fect companion in this transformation journey.

With a big, slobbery lick and a whole lot of doggy love,
Prince

Explore the Dark Side of Dogs Life

Last But Not Least

A Must Have Guidebook for Dog Lovers

Chapter 14

From Worries to Wags

Each breed detail, your dog's explanatory page

Woof woof! Hello, my dear human friend! I've got some exciting news to share. In the upcoming pages, my amazing doggy friends will take the spotlight to tell you about themselves. Get ready to dive into a world of tail-wagging tales and puppy-filled adventures!

You see, every breed has its own unique characteristics that make us special. From how we communicate to our fascinating history and even the things that make us anxious, we're a diverse bunch with much to share. We'll bark about why some breeds have different sounds, how our genetic background influences our behaviors, and what living conditions suit us best.

Whether it's the loyal and lovable Labrador Retriever, the intelligent and regal German Shepherd, the playful and energetic Golden Retriever, or the charming and wrinkly Bulldog, each breed has its own story. From the tiny Chihuahua to the majestic Great Dane, we'll share our experiences, preferences, and what makes us unique.

Some of us may have specific anxieties that need understanding and support. We'll wag our tails as we talk about what makes us nervous and how our loving human companions can help ease our worries. We'll also let you know the secrets to our favorite activities, the amount of sleep we need, and whether we thrive indoors or outdoors.

So, grab a cozy spot on the couch, get ready to cuddle up with your furry friend (that's me!), and turn the page to embark on a delightful journey through the world of dogs. My fellow canine pals will share their stories, insights, and experiences, as if they're speaking directly to you from their wagging mouths.

I can't wait for you to meet them all and discover the extraordinary diversity of our furry family. It will be a howling good time filled with laughter, knowledge, and a deeper understanding of the incredible world of dogs. Let's celebrate the unique bonds between humans and their four-legged companions.

Explore the Dark Side of Dogs Life

Your dog's explanatory page

A Must Have Guidebook for Dog Lovers

Chapter 14

Alaskan Malamute

Woof woof! Hey there, my human buddy! It's your Alaskan Malamute pal, ready to give you the inside scoop on everything you need to know about us magnificent Malamutes.

First things first, let's talk about our breed. Alaskan Malamutes have a fascinating heritage as sled dogs in the Arctic. Bred to be strong, resilient, and friendly, we're like the furry explorers of the dog world! We have an impressive history of pulling heavy loads across snowy terrains and working closely with humans as loyal companions.

Now, let's chat about our unique language of sounds. Oh, the sounds we make are pretty captivating! We have various vocalizations, from our distinctive "woo-woo" howls to our expressive woofs and playful grumbles. When we let out a hearty howl, it's often our way of expressing joy or communicating over long distances. And when we emit a gentle "woo-woo," it's our friendly greeting, saying, "Hey there, I'm here with lots of love to give!"

When it comes to anxiety, us Alaskan Malamutes can sometimes experience uneasiness in certain situations. Loud noises, separation from our loved ones, or unfamiliar environments can make us feel a bit anxious. Providing us with a calm and secure environment, offering comforting reassurance, and gradually introducing us to new experiences will help soothe our worries. Your love, care, and understanding mean the world to us, dear human!

Ah, let's not forget about our likes and dislikes. We Alaskan Malamutes have a natural love for outdoor adventures and physical activities. Whether pulling a sled, going for long hikes, or playing games that stimulate our bodies and minds, we thrive on exercise and exploration. We are adventurous and eager to explore the world alongside our human companions.

Explore the Dark Side of Dogs Life

Your dog's explanatory page

When it's time to unwind, we Malamutes appreciate a cozy spot to rest and rejuvenate. We enjoy curling up in a comfortable spot near a warm fireplace or in a snug dog bed. Our dreamy slumber helps us recharge our energy for the next exciting escapade.

As for living arrangements, we Alaskan Malamutes are versatile and adaptable. While we enjoy spending time indoors with our human pack, we also need access to a secure outdoor area where we can roam, stretch our legs, and breathe fresh air. A spacious yard with a sturdy fence lets us satisfy our natural instincts and stay active.

To ensure our happiness and well-being, owners need to provide us with regular exercise, mental stimulation, and socialization. Positive reinforcement training methods work wonders for us, as we respond well to praise and rewards. A loving and supportive environment, filled with belly rubs and playtime, will make us the happiest Alaskan Malamutes!

In conclusion, dear human, we Alaskan Malamutes are loyal, adventurous, and gentle giants. Our breed's history, unique sounds, and specific needs make us remarkable. We rely on you for love, guidance, and exciting journeys. With your love, patience, and dedication, we'll be the most devoted furry friends you could ever ask for!

So, let's embark on this incredible journey together, my human friend. We'll forge a bond that will withstand the test of time, filled with unforgettable adventures, wagging tails, and endless love. Together, we can conquer the world, one paw at a time!

Sending you big furry hugs and sloppy kisses,
Your Alaskan Malamute

A Must Have Guidebook for Dog Lovers

Chapter 14

Australian Cattle Dog

G'day, mate! Your Australian Cattle Dog buddy is here, ready to give you the lowdown on all things about us energetic and loyal pups. Get ready for a ripper of a time!

First things first, let's talk about our breed. Australian Cattle Dogs, also known as Blue Heelers, are true-blue working dogs. Bred in the land Down Under, we were developed to help farmers herd cattle in the harsh Australian outback. We're known for our intelligence, agility, and unwavering loyalty to our human mates.

Regarding communication, we're not the barkiest of dogs, but we have our own unique way of expressing ourselves. We may give a low, rumbling growl when we're unsure or a sharp, alert bark to let you know something's up. And let's not forget about our expressive eyes! They're like windows to our soul, reflecting our emotions and deep connection with you.

Anxiety can sometimes get the best of us, especially if we're not given enough physical and mental stimulation. We're a breed that craves action and purpose, so providing us with engaging activities, structured training, and plenty of exercises will help keep those anxiety levels at bay. A tired Blue Heeler is a happy Blue Heeler!

Now, let's talk about what gets our tails wagging with excitement. We thrive on mental and physical challenges, so games that require problem-solving or agility exercises are right up our alley. Whether it's learning new tricks, participating in dog sports, or going on adventurous hikes, we're always up for a good time. Oh, and let's not forget about fetch! We're champion fetchers, always ready to chase after that tennis ball or frisbee.

When it comes to sleep, we're not the couch potato types. We're known for our endurance and work ethic, so we're good with around 10 to 12 hours of snooze time each day. But don't be surprised if we're ready to spring back into action at a moment's notice!

Explore the Dark Side of Dogs Life

Your dog's explanatory page

As for living arrangements, we're versatile dogs that can adapt to different environments. However, we thrive in homes with active families who can provide us with ample exercise and mental stimulation. A securely fenced yard is a bonus, as it allows us to explore and burn off our abundant energy.

To keep us happy and healthy, providing us with a balanced diet, regular exercise, and plenty of socialization is important. We're highly trainable and eager to please, so positive reinforcement training methods work best for us. A well-behaved and mentally stimulated Blue Heeler is a contented one!

In conclusion, my dear human companion, we Australian Cattle Dogs are loyal, intelligent, and always up for an adventure. Our working dog background, unique communication style, and energetic nature make us one-of-a-kind. With your love, guidance, and the right amount of mental and physical stimulation, we'll be your faithful and enthusiastic sidekick for life.

So, let's rustle up some fun and create memories that'll last a lifetime! I'm here, by your side, ready to explore the world and shower you with unconditional love and unwavering loyalty.

Cheers and tail wags,
Your Australian Cattle Dog

A Must Have Guidebook for Dog Lovers

Chapter 14

Australian Shepherd

Woof woof! G'day, mate! It's your Australian Shepherd buddy here, ready to give you a glimpse into the amazing world of our breed. Grab your hat, lace up your boots, and get ready for an adventure like no other!

First things first, let's talk about our breed's background. Despite the name, we actually have American roots. Bred to be versatile working dogs, we have a strong herding instinct and a tireless work ethic. Whether it's guiding livestock or mastering agility courses, we're always up for a challenge.

When it comes to communication, we're quite the chatterboxes. We have various vocalizations, from barks and howls to yips and grumbles. Each sound has its meaning, like a secret code between us and our human companions. Listen closely, and you'll understand when we're excited, alerting you to something, or simply saying, "Hey, let's play!"

Anxiety can affect us Australian Shepherds, especially if we don't get enough mental and physical stimulation. We thrive on activity and having a job to do. So, keep us engaged with interactive toys, challenging puzzles, and plenty of exercises. With a consistent routine, positive reinforcement, and lots of love and affection, we'll be your calm and confident sidekick.

Now, let's talk about our likes and dislikes. We're natural athletes, always ready for action. Long walks, hikes in the great outdoors, and even agility training are right up our alley. We're also highly intelligent, so keeping our minds busy with training sessions and learning new tricks will make us wag our tails joyfully. Just be prepared for our playful nature and occasional bursts of zoomies!

When it's time to wind down, we appreciate a cozy relaxing spot. Around 14 to 16 hours of sleep each day is ideal for recharging energy. You might find us curling up on a soft

Explore the Dark Side of Dogs Life

Your dog's explanatory page

bed or claiming a sunny spot by the window. Remember, we're happiest when we balance mental and physical stimulation, so provide us with both.

As for our living arrangements, we're adaptable to different environments. While we can be content in an apartment with regular exercise and mental stimulation, we truly thrive in homes with access to a secure yard where we can stretch our legs and explore. Just make sure the fence is sturdy, as our herding instincts might tempt us to chase after anything that moves!

We need plenty of mental and physical exercise to keep us happy and healthy. Teaching us new tricks, providing challenging puzzles, and engaging in interactive play sessions will keep us mentally stimulated. Regular walks, runs, and off-leash playtime in safe areas will help us burn off energy and maintain our well-being. A tired Aussie is a happy Aussie!

In conclusion, my dear human friend, we Australian Shepherds are energetic, intelligent, and always ready for an adventure. Our unique vocalizations, love for activity, and loyalty make us a breed like no other. With your love, guidance, and plenty of belly rubs, we'll be your most devoted and entertaining companion.

So, let's embark on a thrilling journey together, filled with hikes, training sessions, and unforgettable moments. I'll be by your side, wagging my tail and sporting my signature Aussie grin.

With love and boundless energy,
Your Australian Shepherd

A Must Have Guidebook for Dog Lovers

Chapter 14

Beagle

Woof woof! Hey there, my human buddy! It's your Beagle pal, ready to take you on a sniff-tastic journey to discover everything you need to know about us Beagles. Get ready for a howling good time!

First things first, let's talk about our breed. Beagles are paw-sitively charming and have a rich history as scent hounds. We were originally bred for hunting, using our keen sense of smell to track game. Nowadays, we make paw-some family companions and are known for our friendly and lovable nature.

Now, let's dive into our unique language of sounds. Oh, the sounds we make! We have quite the vocal repertoire, From adorable howls and barks to our expressive whines and bays. When we let out a long, melodic howl, it's often our way of expressing our joy or communicating with other Beagles in the area. And when we emit a series of short, sharp barks, we might alert you to something interesting we've sniffed out!

When it comes to anxiety, we Beagles can sometimes be prone to separation anxiety or get a little anxious when left alone. We thrive on companionship and love being part of the pack. So, keeping us mentally stimulated with interactive toys, puzzles, and plenty of playtime can help alleviate any anxiety we may experience. Your presence and attention mean the world to us!

Now, let's talk about our likes and dislikes. Beagles have a nose for adventure! We love exploring, sniffing everything in sight, and following fascinating scents. Long walks and outdoor adventures are the paw-fect way to keep us happy and healthy. Just remember to keep us on a leash, as our hunting instincts can sometimes lead us astray!

When recharging our batteries, we Beagles need around 12 to 14 hours of sleep daily. So, don't be surprised if you find us curled up in our cozy doggy bed or snoozing in a sunny spot by the window. We take our napping seriously!

Explore the Dark Side of Dogs Life

Your dog's explanatory page

As for living arrangements, we Beagles are adaptable pups. While we can enjoy being indoors with our humans, we also appreciate having access to a secure outdoor area where we can explore and follow our noses. A fenced yard or regular trips to the dog park are tail-waggingly delightful for us!

To ensure our well-being, owners need to provide us with regular exercise, a balanced diet, and mental stimulation. Positive reinforcement training using treats and praise works wonders for us Beagles, as we love learning and pleasing our humans. With patience and consistency, we'll become well-behaved and devoted members of your family pack.

In conclusion, dear human, we Beagles are playful, affectionate, and curious. Our breed's history, unique sounds, and special needs make us special. Remember, we look to you for love, care, and exciting adventures!

So, let's embark on this journey together, my human friend. With your understanding, patience, and lots of belly rubs, we'll create memories that will last a lifetime. Get ready for wagging tails, wet noses, and endless Beagle charm!

Lots of love and wagging tails,
Your Beagle

A Must Have Guidebook for Dog Lovers

Chapter 14

Belgian Malinois

Woof woof! Hey there, my human buddy! It's your Belgian Malinois pal, eager to share all the exciting details about our remarkable breed. Are you ready for an exhilarating adventure? Let's dive right in!

First things first, let's talk about our breed. Belgian Malinois dogs are known for their exceptional intelligence, unwavering loyalty, and impressive work ethic. Originally bred for herding and guarding livestock, we've become versatile working dogs, excelling in various fields such as police work, search and rescue, and even competitive sports. We're like the superheroes of the dog world, ready to tackle any challenge!

Now, let's chat about our unique language of sounds. Oh, the sounds we make are quite fascinating! We have various vocalizations, from sharp barks to soft whines and grunts. When we let out a strong, commanding bark, it's often our way of alerting you to potential dangers or expressing our protective nature. And when we emit gentle, melodic whines, it's our way of communicating our needs and seeking your attention.

When it comes to anxiety, us Belgian Malinois can sometimes experience heightened alertness in certain situations. Our natural protective instincts and high energy levels can make us sensitive to environmental changes. Providing us with mental and physical stimulation, engaging us in challenging tasks, and ensuring a structured routine can help alleviate any anxiety we may feel. Your guidance and support mean the world to us, dear human!

Ah, let's not forget about our likes and dislikes. We Belgian Malinois have an innate drive for activity and purpose. We thrive on mental and physical stimulation, whether it's through obedience training, agility exercises, or engaging in challenging tasks that put our intelligence to the test. We love being your active partners and enjoy having a job to do. Together, we'll conquer any challenge and make every moment count!

Explore the Dark Side of Dogs Life

Your dog's explanatory page

When it's time to rest, we Belgian Malinois appreciate a cozy spot where we can unwind and recharge. A comfortable dog bed or a quiet house corner will do just fine. We may curl up with our favorite toy or simply lay by your side, knowing we're protected and loved.

As for living arrangements, we Belgian Malinois can adapt well to various environments. We appreciate having a space to call our own, indoors, or outdoors. However, providing ample opportunities for exercise and mental stimulation is important, as we have abundant energy to burn. A securely fenced yard and regular outdoor activities will keep us happy and fulfilled.

To ensure our happiness and well-being, owners must provide us with consistent training, socialization, and mental challenges. Positive reinforcement techniques work wonders for us, as we thrive on praise and rewards. A loving and structured environment, coupled with plenty of playtime and affection, will bring out the best in us and strengthen our bond.

In conclusion, dear human, we Belgian Malinois are intelligent, loyal, and driven companions. Our breed's history, unique sounds, and specific needs make us truly exceptional. We look to you for guidance, purpose, and unwavering love. With your dedication, patience, and a dash of adventure, we'll be the most loyal and extraordinary furry friends ever imagined!

So, let's embark on this incredible journey together, my human friend. We'll create a bond that will last a lifetime, filled with unforgettable adventures, wagging tails, and boundless love. Together, we'll conquer the world, one paw at a time!

slobbery kisses and tail wags,
Your Belgian Malinois

A Must Have Guidebook for Dog Lovers

Chapter 14

Bernese Mountain Dog

Woof woof! Hello there, my wonderful human friend! It's your Bernese Mountain Dog buddy, here to share everything you need to know about our paw-sitively amazing breed.

Let's start with our background. We Bernese Mountain Dogs hail from the Swiss Alps, where we were originally bred as working dogs. Our ancestors helped farmers with various tasks, from herding cattle to pulling carts. That's why we have a strong work ethic and a deep sense of loyalty ingrained in our DNA.

When it comes to communication, we may not be the most vocal, but we have our own special ways of expressing ourselves. Our expressive eyes speak volumes, reflecting our gentle and kind nature. And oh, our wagging tails are like a happy flag waving in the breeze, showing our excitement and joy when we're in the company of our beloved humans.

Anxiety can sometimes get the best of us Berners. We're sensitive souls who thrive on love and attention. Thunderstorms, loud noises, or separation from our loved ones can make us anxious. Soothing words, a calm environment, and your reassuring presence can work wonders in calming our worries and making us feel secure and loved.

Now, let's talk about what we love and enjoy. We absolutely adore spending time with our humans, soaking up all the affection and cuddles we can get. We're true gentle giants with a heart as big as the mountains we come from. Long walks in nature, exploring the great outdoors, and feeling the fresh air on our fluffy coats make us wag our tails with pure delight.

When it's time to rest, we appreciate a cozy and comfortable spot to unwind. We typically need around 12 to 14 hours of sleep daily to rejuvenate our bodies and minds.

Explore the Dark Side of Dogs Life

Your dog's explanatory page

You might find us curled up in a favorite corner or stretched out on the floor, dreaming of running through fields and enjoying life's simple pleasures.

As for our living arrangements, we thrive in a home with a yard or access to outdoor space. We love having room to roam and explore, but we also cherish the warmth and comfort of being indoors with our loved ones. A balanced lifestyle with outdoor adventures and quality indoor time will keep us happy and content.

To keep us healthy and fit, regular exercise is important. Daily walks, playtime, and mentally stimulating activities are essential for our well-being. We also appreciate a nutritious diet that supports our active lifestyle. And let's not forget the importance of grooming. Our beautiful, thick coat requires regular brushing to keep it clean and free from tangles.

In conclusion, dear human companion, we Bernese Mountain Dogs are gentle, loyal, and full of love. Our rich heritage, expressive eyes, and unwavering devotion make us incredibly special. With your love, care, and understanding, we'll be the happiest and most devoted furry companions you could ever hope for.

So, let's embark on a journey of love, adventure, and wagging tails. Together, we'll conquer mountains, create cherished memories, and experience a bond that will last a lifetime.

With all my love and loyalty,
Your Bernese Mountain Dog

A Must Have Guidebook for Dog Lovers

Chapter 14

Bichon Frise

Woof woof! Hello, my delightful human friend! Your Bichon Frise pal is here, ready to share all the wonderful things about our fluffy and lovable breed.

Let's start with our background. Bichon Frise is known for our cheerful and affectionate nature. Our rich history dates back to royal courts in the Mediterranean region, where we were adored as companions and performers. Our glamorous white coats and charming personalities made us the darlings of the aristocracy.

Communication is key in any relationship, and we Bichons have our own unique language. We're not the loudest barkers, but we make up for it with our expressive eyes and wagging tails. When we greet you with a bouncy wag and a happy prance, it means we're overjoyed to see you. And when we tilt our heads and give you a curious look, it's our way of saying, "Tell me more, human!"

Anxiety can sometimes get the best of us sensitive Bichons. We may experience separation anxiety when we're away from our beloved humans or when faced with unfamiliar situations. Patience, reassurance, and a consistent routine are crucial in helping us feel secure. Creating a cozy and safe space for us, with familiar scents and comforting toys, can also help ease our worries.

Now, let's talk about what we adore and what makes us wag our tails excitedly. We absolutely love being the center of attention! We thrive on companionship and enjoy being part of a loving family. Cuddles, belly rubs, and gentle strokes are like music to our ears. Daily playtime and interactive toys keep us mentally stimulated and happy.

We're experts in finding the coziest spots when it comes to sleep. We typically need around 12 to 14 hours of sleep daily to recharge our batteries. You might find us curled

Explore the Dark Side of Dogs Life

up on a soft cushion or snuggled under a blanket, dreaming of delightful adventures and delicious treats.

As for living arrangements, we are adaptable little pups who can thrive in various environments. We can happily live in apartments or houses, as long as we have regular walks and playtime to keep us active. While we enjoy our indoor comforts, we also appreciate outdoor strolls and exploring new scents during our daily walks.

To keep us looking our best, regular grooming is essential. Our beautiful white coats require brushing to prevent matting and regular trips to the groomer for trims. A proper diet, high-quality food, and regular veterinary check-ups are important to keep us healthy and happy.

In conclusion, dear human companion, we Bichon Frise are a bundle of joy and love. Our royal heritage, expressive eyes, and affectionate nature make us irresistible. With your love, care, and devotion, we'll be the happiest and most loyal companions you could ever wish for.

So, let's embark on a journey filled with laughter, cuddles, and endless tail wags. Together, we'll create precious memories and share a bond that will warm your heart for years to come.

With all my love and fluffy hugs,
Your Bichon Frise

A Must Have Guidebook for Dog Lovers

Chapter 14

Border Collie

Woof woof! Hello there, my incredible human companion! Your clever and energetic Border Collie buddy is here, ready to share all the paw-some details about our extraordinary breed. Buckle up for a journey into the wonderful world of Border Collies!

Let's start with some breed information. Border Collies are renowned for intelligence, agility, and herding abilities. With our striking coats and captivating eyes, we're quite the eye-catchers. Originally bred as working dogs, our keen instincts and boundless energy make us excellent partners for all sorts of activities.

Now, let's talk about our unique language of sounds. Oh, the sounds we make! From our enthusiastic barks to our excited yips and even our gentle whines, we communicate a wide range of emotions. Listen closely, and you'll understand our distinctive Border Collie language. Each bark, growl, or whimper conveys something meaningful, whether it's signaling excitement, alerting you to something important, or expressing our desire to play and have fun.

When it comes to anxiety, we Border Collies are known to be sensitive souls. Changes in our routine, loud noises, or being left alone for extended periods can sometimes make us feel a bit uneasy. Our humans need to provide us with a stable and secure environment, filled with plenty of mental and physical stimulation. Engaging us in challenging activities, such as puzzle toys or interactive training exercises, can help channel our energy and keep our minds occupied. Your patience, understanding, and loving presence mean the world to us during moments of anxiety.

Ah, let's not forget about our likes and dislikes. We Border Collies absolutely adore having a job to do! Whether it's herding sheep, fetching a frisbee, or participating in dog sports like agility or flyball, we thrive on mental and physical challenges. We're happiest when we have a purpose and an opportunity to showcase our intelligence and athleticism.

Explore the Dark Side of Dogs Life

Your dog's explanatory page

Don't be surprised if we give you that intense stare, eagerly waiting for the next exciting adventure!

When it's time to wind down, we appreciate a cozy spot to relax and recharge. While our sleep needs may vary, we generally require 12 to 14 hours of restful slumber daily. So, you might find us snuggled up on a soft dog bed or curling up at your feet, dreaming of chasing squirrels or mastering new tricks.

As for living arrangements, we Border Collies can adapt well to different environments as long as we have plenty of mental and physical stimulation. While we appreciate access to a secure outdoor area where we can stretch our legs and indulge in playful activities, we also cherish our time indoors with our beloved humans. A combination of stimulating exercises, challenging games, and interactive training sessions will help keep us happy and content.

We must have regular exercise, mental stimulation, and socialization to ensure our well-being. We thrive on activities that engage our minds and bodies, such as long walks, obedience training, and interactive playtime. A routine that incorporates both physical exercise and mental challenges will help us be the happiest and healthiest Border Collies we can be.

In conclusion, dear human, we Border Collies are intelligent, agile, and bursting with energy. Our unique language, herding heritage, and loving nature make us truly special companions. With your guidance, patience, and plenty of playtime, we'll be the happiest Border Collies on the planet!

So, let's embark on a lifetime of adventures together, filled with wagging tails, endless games of fetch, and a bond that will make our hearts soar. Get ready for an extraordinary journey alongside your incredible Border Collie companion!

Lots of love and boundless energy,
Your Border Collie

A Must Have Guidebook for Dog Lovers

Chapter 14

Boston Terrier

Woof woof! Hey there, my awesome human friend! It's your spunky and spirited Boston Terrier buddy, here to fill you in on all the delightful details about our fantastic breed. Get ready for a paws-itively fun adventure!

Let's start with our breed's background. Boston Terriers, also known as the American Gentlemen, were originally bred in the United States. With our tuxedo-like markings and charming personalities, we're the life of the party wherever we go. We're a small package with a big heart!

Now, let's talk about our unique language of sounds. We may not be the most talkative pups, but we sure know how to make ourselves heard. We have a wide range of expressive sounds conveying everything from excitement to curiosity. Listen closely to our happy snorts, adorable grumbles, and occasional barks, as they're our way of communicating with you and the world around us.

When it comes to anxiety, we Boston Terriers are known for being sensitive souls. Loud noises, changes in routine, or being left alone for long periods can make us feel a bit anxious. Creating a calm and comforting environment, providing plenty of mental and physical stimulation, and showering us with love and attention will help ease our worries. Your presence and gentle reassurance mean the world to us!

Ah, let's not forget about our likes and dislikes. Boston Terriers is full of energy and enthusiasm! We absolutely love spending quality time with our favorite humans. Whether it's playing fetch in the park, going on exciting walks, or snuggling up on the couch for some cuddle time, we thrive on the love and companionship you provide.

When it's time to recharge our batteries, we appreciate a cozy spot to rest and relax. We typically need around 12 to 14 hours of snooze time each day to keep our energetic spirits

Explore the Dark Side of Dogs Life

Your dog's explanatory page

high. So, don't be surprised if you find us curled up in the coziest corner of the house, catching some Z's and dreaming of fun-filled adventures.

As for living arrangements, we Boston Terriers are quite adaptable. We can thrive in various settings, whether it's a bustling city apartment or a spacious suburban home. Remember that we're sensitive to extreme temperatures, so make sure we have a cool and comfortable place to relax during hot summer days.

To ensure our well-being, it's important to provide us with regular exercise and mental stimulation. Daily walks, playtime, and interactive toys will keep us physically and mentally fit. And don't forget to maintain our adorable bat ears and keep them clean to prevent any pesky ear infections.

In conclusion, dear human, we Boston Terriers are lively, loving, and always up for a good time. Our unique history, expressive sounds, and playful nature make us truly special. With your love, care, and attention to our needs, we'll be the happiest little companions you could ever ask for.

So, let's embark on a lifetime of adventures together, filled with laughter, wagging tails, and unconditional love. Get ready for a bond that will bring you endless joy and smiles!

Lots of love and slobbery kisses,
Your Boston Terrier

A Must Have Guidebook for Dog Lovers

Chapter 14

137

Boxer

Woof woof! Hey there, my human buddy! It's your Boxer buddy here, ready to bounce into your life and share everything you need to know about us Boxers. Get ready for a tail-wagging good time!

First things first, let's talk about our breed. Boxers are known for our strong, muscular bodies and expressive faces. We have a playful and energetic nature, making us excellent companions for active families. We're often described as the "Peter Pan" of the dog world because we never seem to outgrow our puppy-like enthusiasm.

Now, let's dive into our unique language of sounds. We Boxers are quite vocal! We communicate with a variety of barks, grunts, and even "woo-woo" noises. When we emit a series of short barks, it's usually our way of saying, "Hey, let's play!" And when we make those adorable woo-woo sounds, it's our way of expressing excitement and happiness.

When it comes to anxiety, some Boxers can be prone to separation anxiety. We form strong bonds with our humans and can feel anxious when left alone for extended periods. Providing plenty of exercise, mental stimulation, and a comfortable and secure environment can help ease our worries. Remember, we thrive on love and attention, so shower us with affection!

Let's talk about our likes and dislikes. Boxers are known for our love of play and activity. We have a high energy level and need plenty of exercise to keep us happy and healthy. Play fetch with us, take us for long walks, and engage us in interactive games—it's a great way to channel our energy and keep us entertained.

Explore the Dark Side of Dogs Life

Your dog's explanatory page

When it's time to rest, we Boxers appreciate a cozy spot to curl up in. We may choose a soft doggy bed or even your lap for our nap time. We love being close to our humans, so expect lots of snuggles and warm cuddles when we're ready to relax.

As for living arrangements, Boxers are adaptable and can thrive in various environments. While we enjoy being indoors with our family, we also love exploring and playing outdoors. Access to a secure yard or regular trips to the dog park can be a Boxer's dream come true. Just make sure to keep an eye on us, as we can be curious and sometimes mischievous!

To ensure our well-being, owners need to provide us with regular exercise, mental stimulation, and consistent training. Positive reinforcement techniques work best for us, as we respond well to praise and rewards. Socialization is also key, as it helps us become well-rounded and confident dogs.

In conclusion, dear human, we Boxers are energetic, playful, and full of love. Our breed's unique sounds, needs, and affectionate nature make us truly special. Remember, we look to you for love, care, and exciting adventures!

So, let's embark on this journey together, my human friend. With your patience, understanding, and lots of belly rubs, we'll create a bond that will last a lifetime. Get ready for wagging tails, slobbery kisses, and a whole lot of Boxer love!

Lots of love and slobbery kisses,
Your Boxer

A Must Have Guidebook for Dog Lovers

Chapter 14

Brittany

Woof woof! Hello there, my human friend! It's your Brittany buddy, excited to tell you all about our wonderful breed.

First things first, let's talk about our breed. Brittany is known for their boundless energy, intelligence, and friendly nature. Originally bred as hunting dogs, we're natural athletes and love being active partners in all your outdoor pursuits. Whether it's hiking, running, or playing fetch, we're always up for a thrilling adventure by your side!

Now, let's chat about our unique language of sounds. Oh, the sounds we make are quite delightful! We have an array of barks, chirps, and excited yips that we use to communicate our joy and enthusiasm. When we let out a high-pitched bark, it's our way of saying, "Hey, let's play!" And when we emit soft whines and gentle growls, it might mean we're feeling affectionate or seeking your attention.

When it comes to anxiety, us Brittany can sometimes get a little restless if we don't get enough mental and physical stimulation. We thrive on activities that challenge our minds and bodies, so keeping us engaged with puzzle toys, obedience training, and interactive play sessions is key to keeping us happy and content. Your love and companionship mean the world to us, dear human!

Ah, let's not forget about our likes and dislikes. We Brittany absolutely adores being outdoors and exploring the world with our curious noses. We have a natural instinct for hunting and scent tracking, so providing us with opportunities to engage in these activities will make us feel fulfilled. We also have a soft spot for cuddling and belly rubs, as they make us feel safe and loved. When it's time to rest, we Brittany appreciates a cozy spot where we can curl up and recharge. A soft dog bed or a sunny spot by the window will do just fine. We may snooze with a toy by our side or nuzzle up against you, knowing that we're cherished members of your pack.

Explore the Dark Side of Dogs Life

Your dog's explanatory page

As for living arrangements, we Brittany are versatile and can adapt well to different environments. While we enjoy having access to a secure outdoor space where we can stretch our legs, we also cherish our time indoors with our beloved human family. Daily exercise and mental stimulation are crucial for our well-being, so regular walks, playtime, and training sessions are a must!

To ensure our happiness and well-being, owners need to provide us with plenty of exercise, mental challenges, and positive reinforcement training. We thrive on praise and rewards, so be generous with your encouragement and treats! A loving and nurturing environment, filled with play, affection, and exciting adventures, will make us the happiest Brittany on the planet!

In conclusion, dear human, we Brittany are energetic, intelligent, and loving companions. Our breed's history, unique sounds, and specific needs make us truly special. We rely on you for guidance, love, and thrilling escapades. With your care, dedication, and a sprinkle of adventure, we'll be the most loyal and joyful furry friends you could ever have!

So, let's embark on this incredible journey together, my human friend. We'll create memories, share laughter, and forge an unbreakable bond that will last a lifetime. Get ready for a whirlwind of wagging tails, endless fun, and pure canine love!

Sending you love and wagging tails,
Your Brittany

A Must Have Guidebook for Dog Lovers

Bulldog (English/French)

Woof woof! Hey there, my human buddy! It's your Bulldog pal, ready to share all the woof-tastic details about us English and French Bulldogs. Get ready for a bulldozer of cuteness and charm!

First things first, let's talk about our breed. Bulldogs are known for our distinctive appearance and lovable personalities. English Bulldogs have a rich history as fierce bull-baiting dogs turned gentle companions. French Bulldogs, on the other paw, were bred as companion dogs from English Bulldogs. We're like adorable little bundles of wrinkly goodness!

Now, let's talk about our unique language of sounds. Oh, the sounds we make! We have quite the vocal range from our adorable snorts and snores to our low grumbles and barks. When we emit a playful snort or a funny snore, it means we're content and relaxed. And when we let out a short, sharp bark, it's our way of saying, "Hey, let's have some fun!"

When it comes to anxiety, we Bulldogs can sometimes be sensitive souls. We may experience separation anxiety or get anxious in unfamiliar or noisy environments. Providing us with a calm, secure space, plenty of snuggles, and a consistent routine can help ease our worries. Your loving presence and gentle reassurance mean the world to us!

Now, let's talk about our likes and dislikes. Bulldogs may have a reputation for being a bit lazy, but we still enjoy our playtime and walks. Remember that we have a moderate exercise need due to our unique physique. Short walks and fun indoor games that don't strain our breathing are the paw-fect way to keep us happy and healthy!

When it's time to catch some z's, we Bulldogs are expert snoozers. We need around 12 to 14 hours of sleep daily to recharge our wrinkly batteries. So, don't be surprised if you

Explore the Dark Side of Dogs Life

find us snoring away in our favorite cozy corner or sprawling out on the comfiest spot in the house. We take napping to a whole new level!

As for our living arrangements, Bulldogs are quite adaptable. While we enjoy being indoors where we can be close to our humans, we also appreciate some outdoor time to explore and sniff around. Remember that we're not the best swimmers, so be cautious around water.

To ensure our well-being, owners must provide us with a balanced diet, regular vet check-ups, and proper grooming to keep our adorable wrinkles clean and healthy. Additionally, positive reinforcement training using treats and praise works wonders for us Bulldogs. We may have a stubborn streak, but we'll become well-behaved and loyal companions with patience and love.

In conclusion, dear human, we Bulldogs are bundles of love, charm, and wrinkly delight. Our breed's history, unique sounds, and special needs make us truly one-of-a-kind. Remember, we rely on you for care, love, and belly rubs galore!

So, let's embark on this adventure together, my human friend. We'll create a lifetime bond with your understanding, patience, and lots of slobbery kisses. Get ready for endless moments of cuteness and bulldog snuggles!

Lots of love and adorable snorts,
Your Bulldog

A Must Have Guidebook for Dog Lovers

Chapter 14

Cane Corso

Woof woof! Hey there, my human pal! It's your Cane Corso buddy, eager to share everything about our amazing breed. Are you ready for an adventure filled with strength, loyalty, and love? Let's dive right in!

First things first, let's talk about our breed. Cane Corso are known for their majestic appearance and powerful physique. We exude confidence and are natural protectors. Originally bred as working dogs, we have a strong sense of loyalty and a deep bond with our human families. We're like gentle giants with hearts of gold!

Now, let's chat about our unique language of sounds. Oh, the sounds we make are quite intriguing! We have a deep, rumbling bark that can send shivers down the spine of intruders. It's our way of saying, "Hey, I've got this. You're safe with me!" We're also masters of body language, using our expressive eyes and stance to communicate our emotions and intentions.

When it comes to anxiety, us Cane Corso can sometimes be sensitive souls. We thrive on a calm and stable environment; sudden changes or unfamiliar situations can make us feel uneasy. Offering us a safe and secure space, maintaining consistent routines, and showering us with gentle affection can help alleviate any anxieties we may experience. Your understanding and reassurance mean the world to us, dear human!

Ah, let's not forget about our likes and dislikes. We Cane Corso love spending quality time with our humans. Whether it's going for long walks, playing in the backyard, or just relaxing by your side, we cherish every moment we get to be in your company. We have a protective nature and knowing that we're keeping you safe and loved brings us immense joy.

When it's time to rest, we Cane Corso appreciate a cozy spot where we can curl up and unwind. A soft bed or a quiet corner will be our retreat, as we recharge our energy for the

Explore the Dark Side of Dogs Life

adventures that await. We may snore a little, but that's just a sign of contentment and relaxation.

As for living arrangements, we Cane Corso are versatile and adaptable. While we enjoy having access to a secure outdoor area where we can stretch our muscles, we also appreciate being close to our human family indoors. We thrive on love, attention, and guidance. Regular exercise and mental stimulation are essential for our well-being, so engaging in activities that challenge us physically and mentally is important.

To ensure our happiness and well-being, owners must provide us with proper socialization, positive reinforcement training, and a strong leadership role. We respond well to consistent boundaries and clear communication. We'll become well-rounded and confident companions with your patient guidance and firm yet gentle approach.

In conclusion, dear human, we Cane Corso are loyal, protective, and loving companions. Our breed's history, unique sounds, and specific needs make us truly special. We rely on you for love, guidance, and a sense of purpose. With your unwavering support, we'll be the most devoted and fearless furry friends you could ever ask for!

So, let's embark on this incredible journey together, my human friend. We'll create an unbreakable bond, filled with cherished memories, and a love that knows no bounds. Get ready for a lifetime of adventure, loyalty, and endless tail wags!

Sending you big, warm Cane Corso hugs,
Your Cane Corso

A Must Have Guidebook for Dog Lovers

Chapter 14

Cardigan Welsh Corgi

Woof woof! Hey there, my human friend! It's your Cardigan Welsh Corgi buddy, ready to share all the delightful details about our wonderful breed. Are you ready for a tail-wagging adventure? Let's jump right in!

First things first, let's talk about our breed. Cardigan Welsh Corgis are small in size but big in personality! With our adorable long bodies and short legs, we're quite the charming companions. Originally bred as herding dogs, we're intelligent, alert, and always eager to please. We may be small, but we have hearts full of love and loyalty!

Now, let's chat about our unique language of sounds. Oh, the sounds we make are quite fascinating! We have a variety of vocalizations, from barks and yips to playful growls and even a unique "woo-woo" sound that's all our own. Each sound communicates our emotions, whether it's excitement, alertness, or just wanting your attention.

Regarding anxiety, we Cardigan Welsh Corgis can be sensitive souls. Loud noises, unfamiliar surroundings, or separation from our loved ones can make us feel a little anxious. But fear not, dear human, as your reassuring presence and a calm environment can work wonders in soothing our worries. A gentle touch, a kind word, and creating a safe haven for us will help us feel secure and loved.

Ah, let's not forget about our likes and dislikes. We Cardigan Welsh Corgis are known for our playful nature and boundless energy. We love engaging in activities that stimulate both our minds and bodies. Whether it's going for walks, playing fetch, or participating in fun training sessions, we thrive on the joy of being active and involved in your daily life. Don't be surprised if we try to herd you or anything that moves, it's in our nature! When it's time to rest, we appreciate a cozy spot to curl up and recharge.

Explore the Dark Side of Dogs Life

Your dog's explanatory page

Our favorite nap zone will be a soft bed, a warm blanket, or even your lap. We may even tuck our little tails close to our bodies to keep warm and snug. After a good rest, we'll be ready for more adventures and wagging tails!

As for living arrangements, we Cardigan Welsh Corgis adapt well to both indoor and outdoor environments. Although we may be small, we still require regular exercise to keep our bodies and minds healthy. A securely fenced yard or supervised playtime in a safe area allows us to explore and burn off our energy. But remember, we're also social creatures who want to be near our human pack, so indoor time with you is just as important.

To ensure our happiness and well-being, owners must provide us with mental stimulation, positive reinforcement training, and lots of love. We thrive on your guidance and appreciate consistent boundaries. With your patient and kind approach, we'll become well-rounded companions and bring you endless joy.

In conclusion, dear human, we Cardigan Welsh Corgis are loving, lively, and loyal friends. Our breed's history, unique sounds, and specific needs make us truly special. We rely on you for love, guidance, and a sense of purpose. With your companionship and care, we'll be the happiest and most devoted furry friends you could ever have!

So, let's embark on this incredible journey together, my human friend. We'll create a bond that's filled with joy, laughter, and unforgettable moments. Get ready for a lifetime of wagging tails and Corgi smiles!

Sending you Corgi kisses and wagging tails,
Your Cardigan Welsh Corgi

A Must Have Guidebook for Dog Lovers

Chapter 14

Cavalier King Charles Spaniel

Woof woof! Hello, my dear human companion! It's your loyal and affectionate Cavalier King Charles Spaniel here, ready to take you on a tail-wagging adventure into the world of our delightful breed.

Let's start with a little history. We Cavaliers have a regal lineage that traces back to the courts of King Charles I and King Charles II in England. We were cherished as companions by nobles and royalty, and that's where our love for human companionship and affectionate nature originates. We're often described as "love sponges" because we soak up all the love and attention you give us!

When it comes to communication, we have a language of our own. We may not bark excessively, but we have expressive eyes that can instantly melt your heart. Our gentle, soulful gazes can convey a range of emotions, from excitement and happiness to longing and curiosity. And let's not forget about our endearing little whimper when we want something!

Anxiety can be a concern for us sensitive Cavaliers. We thrive on love and can feel uneasy when left alone for long periods. Our humans need to provide us with plenty of companionship and create a secure environment for us. Gentle reassurance, positive reinforcement training, and keeping a consistent routine can help alleviate our worries and keep us calm and content.

Now, let's talk about our likes and dislikes. We absolutely adore being near our humans and crave your attention. Cuddling up on your lap or snuggling beside you on the couch is pure bliss for us. We also enjoy leisurely walks in the park, exploring new scents, and taking in the sights and sounds of nature. Just be careful not to overexert us, as we're not the most athletic of breeds.

Explore the Dark Side of Dogs Life

Your dog's explanatory page

When it's time to rest, we appreciate our beauty sleep. We typically need around 12 to 14 hours of sleep daily to recharge our batteries. You'll often find us nestled in a cozy spot, dreaming of chasing butterflies or simply enjoying the warmth of your presence. Our peaceful slumbers rejuvenate us and prepare us for more adventures by your side.

As for our living arrangements, we adapt well to various environments. Whether it's a spacious house or a cozy apartment, we're adaptable and thrive on the love and attention we receive from our humans. We enjoy indoor and outdoor activities but should always be supervised outdoors to ensure our safety.

We must have a nutritious diet and regular exercise to keep us healthy and happy. We may tend to gain weight, so portion control and a balanced diet are important. Regular grooming, including brushing our silky coat and cleaning our ears, will help us look and feel our best. And, of course, lots of love, cuddles, and gentle playtime will make us the happiest Cavaliers in the world.

In conclusion, my dear human friend, we Cavaliers are gentle, loving, and loyal companions. Our regal history, expressive eyes, and unwavering devotion make us truly special. With your love, care, and understanding, we'll be by your side, wagging our tails and showering you with endless love and joy.

So, let's embark on a journey of shared adventures and heartwarming moments. I'll be there, wagging my tail and melting your heart with every loving gaze.

With all my love and devotion,
Your Cavalier King Charles Spaniel

A Must Have Guidebook for Dog Lovers

Chihuahua

Woof woof! Hey there, my tiny human buddy! It's your Chihuahua pal here, ready to share all the woof-tastic details about us Chihuahuas. Get ready for a pint-sized adventure!

Let's start by talking about our breed. Chihuahuas are small but mighty! We may be tiny in size, but we have big personalities. Originating from Mexico, we are known for our alertness and courageous nature. Don't let our small stature fool you—we have a big heart and plenty of love to give.

Now, let's chat about our unique language of sounds. Oh, the sounds we make! We have a range of barks, yips, and even howls. When we bark rapidly and insistently, it's usually our way of saying, "Hey, pay attention to me!" And when we let out a high-pitched howl, it might be our way of expressing excitement or joining in on the neighborhood choir.

When it comes to anxiety, some Chihuahuas can be prone to nervousness. We may get anxious when meeting unfamiliar people or animals in new situations. Providing us with a calm and secure environment is essential. Be patient and offer reassurance during these moments, as we look to you for comfort and safety.

Let's talk about our likes and dislikes. Chihuahuas adore being the center of attention! We love cuddling up in your lap, basking in your love and affection. Being social butterflies, we enjoy meeting new people and other friendly dogs. But remember, due to our small size, we prefer gentle play and interactions.

When it's time to rest, we Chihuahuas are experts at finding cozy spots. We love burrowing under blankets or snuggling in our favorite doggy bed. Creating a comfortable and warm space for us to relax is a paw-some way to make us feel secure and loved.

Your dog's explanatory page

As for living arrangements, Chihuahuas can adapt well to both indoor and outdoor environments. We're perfectly suited for apartment living as long as we get plenty of mental and physical stimulation. However, since we are small and delicate, keeping us safe and supervising us outdoors is important. We can easily be spooked by larger dogs or fast-moving objects.

To ensure our well-being, owners need to provide us with regular exercise, mental stimulation, and socialization. We may be small, but we still need our daily walks and playtime to keep us happy and healthy. Positive reinforcement training methods work best for us, as we respond well to praise and rewards.

In conclusion, dear human, we Chihuahuas are little bundles of joy. Our breed's unique sounds, needs, and affectionate nature make us truly special. Remember, we may be small, but our love for you is immeasurable.

So, let's embark on this adventure together, my tiny human friend. With your love, care, and plenty of belly rubs, we'll create a bond that will last a lifetime. Get ready for big smiles, sassy attitudes, and a whole lot of Chihuahua love!

Lots of love and slobbery kisses,
Your Chihuahua

A Must Have Guidebook for Dog Lovers

Chapter 14

Cocker Spaniel

Woof woof! Hello, my wonderful human companion! Your loyal and cheerful Cocker Spaniel's buddy is here, ready to wag my tail and share all the fantastic things about our paw-some breed. Get ready for a delightful journey into the world of Cocker Spaniels!

Let's start with a little background information. We Cocker Spaniels have a rich history as hunting dogs, known for our remarkable scenting abilities and skills in flushing out game birds. But don't let that fool you! We're not just outdoor enthusiasts but also loving and affectionate family companions.

Now, let's talk about our unique language of sounds. Oh, the sounds we make! We have quite the vocal range from our friendly barks to our charming whimpering and even the occasional adorable howl. We use these sounds to communicate our excitement, happiness, and sometimes our need for attention or playtime. Just listen closely, and you'll understand our joyful Cocker Spaniel language!

When it comes to anxiety, we Cocker Spaniels can sometimes be sensitive souls. Loud noises, unfamiliar environments, or being separated from our loved ones can make us a bit anxious. Offering us a calm and secure environment, providing comforting reassurance, and engaging us in interactive play or training can help ease our worries. Your loving presence means the world to us, and it's our greatest comfort during those anxious moments.

Ah, let's not forget about our likes and dislikes. We Cocker Spaniels absolutely adore being active and exploring the world around us! Going for walks, playing fetch, or participating in agility training are all fantastic ways to keep us mentally and physically stimulated. We also cherish quality cuddle time with you, as we thrive on your love and attention.

Explore the Dark Side of Dogs Life

Your dog's explanatory page

When it's time to wind down, we appreciate our cozy naptime. We typically need around 12 to 14 hours of restful sleep daily to recharge our energy. So, don't be surprised if you find us curled up in our favorite dog bed or snuggled up next to you on the couch, dreaming of chasing butterflies and wagging our tails with delight.

As for living arrangements, we Cocker Spaniels can adapt well to both indoor and outdoor environments. We're versatile pups who can thrive in various settings, but we truly value being close to our beloved humans. Whether it's a spacious backyard to explore or a comfortable home with cozy corners, we'll be happy and content if we have your love and attention.

To ensure our well-being, it's essential to provide us with regular exercise, mental stimulation, and socialization. We enjoy daily walks or play sessions to burn off our abundant energy. Grooming is also an important part of our care routine, as our beautiful coats require regular brushing and occasional trips to the groomer to keep us looking our best.

In conclusion, dear human, we Cocker Spaniels are bundles of love, joy, and enthusiasm. Our hunting heritage, unique sounds, and affectionate nature make us truly special companions. With your care, attention, and plenty of belly rubs, we'll be the happiest Cocker Spaniels in the world!

So, let's embark on a lifetime of unforgettable adventures together, filled with wagging tails, wet kisses, and unconditional love. Get ready for a bond that will warm your heart and bring endless joy to your life!

Lots of love and wagging tails,
Your Cocker Spaniel

A Must Have Guidebook for Dog Lovers

Chapter 14

Dachshund

Woof woof! Hello there, my human buddy! Your Dachshund pal is here to give you the lowdown on everything you need to know about us Doxies. Get ready for a tail-wagging good time!

First things first, let's talk about our breed. We Dachshunds are small dogs with a long body and short legs. We were originally bred in Germany to hunt badgers, which is why we have a strong and determined nature. We may be pint-sized, but we have the heart of a mighty hunter!

Now, let's dig into our unique language of sounds. Oh, the sounds we make! We have quite the vocal range, from deep and expressive barks to adorable howls. When we let out short and sharp barks, it's often our way of alerting you to something interesting or suspicious. And when we unleash our melodic howls, we might be expressing our joy or calling out to our fellow furry friends.

When it comes to anxiety, some Dachshunds can be prone to worry. Loud noises or sudden environmental changes can make us a little nervous. Soothing us with gentle words, providing a safe and cozy den for us to retreat to, and offering comforting touches can work wonders in calming our worries. Remember, we rely on you to be our anchor of reassurance!

Now, let's talk about our likes and dislikes. We Dachshunds are playful and adventurous pups! We love exploring the world around us, whether it's chasing after squirrels or digging in the backyard. We also have a knack for burrowing and tunneling, so creating a designated digging area or providing us with cozy blankets to snuggle under will make us wag our tails with delight.

When it's time to rest those short little legs, we Dachshunds appreciate a comfy spot to curl up in. We love finding the coziest corners of the house or nestling into a plush doggy

Explore the Dark Side of Dogs Life

bed. Offering us a warm and inviting space for our snooze time is a paw-some way to show us your love.

As for living arrangements, Dachshunds are adaptable and can thrive in various settings. Whether you live in a cozy apartment or a spacious house with a backyard, we can make ourselves at home. However, it's important to note that we must be handled with care due to our long backs to avoid potential back problems. So, gentle play and avoiding activities that put strain on our spines are essential.

To ensure our well-being, owners need to provide us with regular exercise, mental stimulation, and socialization. Daily walks, interactive toys, and puzzle games will keep our curious minds engaged. Positive reinforcement training methods work wonders for us, as we are eager to please and respond well to praise and rewards.

In conclusion, dear human, we Dachshunds are spirited, loyal, and full of character. Our breed's unique sounds, needs, and determination make us truly special. With your love, care, and a whole lot of belly rubs, we'll be the happiest little sausage dogs around!

So, let's embark on this adventure together, my human friend. With your guidance and endless affection, we'll create memories that will warm our hearts for years. Get ready for wagging tails, wet nose kisses, and a whole lot of Dachshund charm!

Lots of love and slobbery kisses,
Your Dachshund

A Must Have Guidebook for Dog Lovers

Chapter 14

Doberman Pinscher

Woof woof! Hello there, my fearless and devoted human friend! It's your loyal Doberman Pinscher pal, ready to unveil the fascinating world of our remarkable breed. Get ready for an adventure filled with loyalty, strength, and endless love!

Let's start with some breed information. We Doberman Pinschers are renowned for our sleek and muscular appearance. We're quite the head-turners with our velvety coats, striking colors, and alert ears. Bred as versatile working dogs, we possess a unique blend of intelligence, athleticism, and unwavering loyalty.

Now, let's talk about our communication style. We Dobermans have a wide range of vocal expressions. From deep and authoritative barks to playful woofs and gentle howls, we use our voice to convey our emotions. When we bark with a strong and commanding tone, it's often to alert you of potential danger or protect our beloved humans. And when we let out joyful yips and excited whines, it's our way of saying, "Let's play and have some fun!"

Anxiety can sometimes affect us Dobermans, especially if we lack mental and physical stimulation. We thrive on regular exercise, mental challenges, and, most importantly, your loving presence. Spending quality time with us, engaging in interactive games, and ensuring a structured routine will help alleviate any anxiety we may experience. We look up to you as our trusted leader and protector, so your calm and reassuring presence is key to our happiness and well-being.

Let's not forget about our likes and dislikes. We Dobermans have an innate drive to protect and serve our families. We're devoted and fiercely loyal, always ready to stand by your side. Our favorite activities include engaging in obedience training, participating in dog sports like agility or scent work, and even snuggling up with you on the couch.

Explore the Dark Side of Dogs Life

Your dog's explanatory page

We cherish our time with you; any opportunity for physical exercise and mental stimulation will make us wag our tails with joy!

When it's time to rest, we appreciate a cozy and comfortable spot to recharge our batteries. Although our sleep needs may vary, we generally require around 10 to 12 hours of rest each day. So, you may find us curled up in our favorite bed or sleeping contentedly in a quiet corner of the house, dreaming of exciting adventures and endless cuddles.

As for our living arrangements, we Dobermans can adapt to various environments, as long as we receive proper care, training, and exercise. While we appreciate a secure outdoor area where we can stretch our legs and explore, we're also content living indoors with our beloved humans. Remember, we thrive on being an integral part of your daily life, so including us in your activities and ensuring we receive ample mental and physical stimulation will bring out the best in us.

To ensure our well-being, owners need to provide us with regular exercise, mental challenges, and socialization from an early age. We Dobermans are intelligent and eager to please, making us excellent candidates for obedience training and advanced activities. Positive reinforcement methods, consistency, and clear boundaries will help us grow into well-rounded and happy companions.

In conclusion, dear human, we Doberman Pinschers are the epitome of loyalty, strength, and unwavering love. Our unique communication style, protective instincts, and athleticism make us truly special companions. With your guidance, love, and plenty of belly rubs, we'll be the happiest Dobermans on the planet!

Lots of love and unwavering devotion,
Your Doberman Pinscher

A Must Have Guidebook for Dog Lovers

Chapter 14

English Cocker

Woof woof! Hello there, my human friend! It's your English Cocker pal, ready to share all the woof-tastic details about our fabulous breed. Are you ready to dive into the world of English Cocker? Let's get started!

First things first, let's talk about our breed. English Cocker is renowned for our charm, intelligence, and playful nature. We're medium-sized dogs with beautiful, expressive eyes and soft, silky coats that make us irresistible. Originally bred as hunting companions, we have a natural talent for sniffing out the game and retrieving it with enthusiasm.

Now, let's chat about our unique language of sounds. We're quite vocal and expressive! We use a range of delightful sounds, from soft whines to excited barks, to communicate our emotions and desires. When we wag our tails rapidly and let out a joyful bark, it means we're bursting with excitement and happiness. And when we give you those soulful puppy dog eyes, it's our way of saying, "I love you!"

When it comes to anxiety, we English Cocker can be sensitive souls. Changes in routine, loud noises, or separation from our loved ones can make us feel a little anxious. But fear not, dear human, as your love and reassurance are the keys to calming our worries. Your gentle touch, soothing words, and secure environment will make us feel safe and secure.

Ah, let's not forget about our likes and dislikes. We English Cocker are active and energetic dogs who love to explore and play. We thrive on engaging in activities that challenge our minds and keep us physically active. Whether going for long walks, playing fetch in the park, or participating in obedience training, we're always up for some fun and adventure. Plus, a good belly rub and cuddle session with you will make our tails wag with delight!

When it's time to relax, we appreciate a cozy spot to curl up and unwind. A soft bed or a comfy couch will be our favorite place to take a nap and recharge our batteries. We

Explore the Dark Side of Dogs Life

may even snuggle up close to you for extra warmth and comfort. After a refreshing rest, we'll be ready to join you for more exciting escapades!

As for living arrangements, we English Cocker adapt well to indoor and outdoor environments. We enjoy spending quality time with our human pack, so being indoors with you is important. However, we also appreciate outdoor activities and require regular exercise to keep us happy and healthy. Whether it's exploring a secure backyard or going on adventures with you, we'll be thrilled to have a balance of indoor and outdoor experiences.

To ensure our well-being and happiness, owners must provide us with mental stimulation, regular exercise, and lots of love. Positive reinforcement training methods work wonders for us, as we respond well to praise and rewards. A structured routine, socialization with other dogs, and plenty of playtime will make us wag our tails with delight.

In conclusion, dear human, we English Cocker are loving, intelligent, and playful companions. Our breed's unique characteristics, expressive sounds, and specific needs make us truly special. With your love, care, and companionship, we'll be the happiest and most devoted furry friends you could ever ask for!

So, let's embark on this delightful journey together, my human friend. We'll create memories that will last a lifetime, filled with wagging tails, wet kisses, and endless joy. Get ready for a paw-some adventure with your English Cocker companion!

Sending you joyful spaniel kisses and wagging tails,
Your English Cocker

A Must Have Guidebook for Dog Lovers

Chapter 14

English Setter

Woof woof! Greetings, my fantastic human companion! It's your loyal and playful English Setter pal here, excited to share all the amazing things about our wonderful breed. Get ready for a tail-wagging journey into the world of English Setters!

Let's start with a little background information. We English Setters have a fascinating history as versatile hunting dogs, known for our exceptional scenting abilities and graceful movement. Our elegant, feathered coat and natural hunting instincts make us a sight to behold and a joy to have by your side.

Now, let's talk about our unique language of sounds. Oh, the sounds we make! We have quite the vocal range from our friendly barks to our melodious howls and even our expressive whines. We use these sounds to communicate our excitement, curiosity, and sometimes our desire for adventure or playtime. Just listen closely, and you'll understand our charming English Setter language!

When it comes to anxiety, we English Setters are generally easygoing and adaptable. However, situations like being left alone for extended periods or experiencing sudden changes in our routine can make us a bit anxious. Providing us with a secure and comforting environment, engaging us in interactive activities, and offering mental stimulation through puzzle toys or training exercises can help alleviate any anxiety we may feel. Your loving presence and reassurance mean the world to us!

Ah, let's not forget about our likes and dislikes. We English Setters absolutely love being outdoors and exploring nature's wonders! Whether it's going for long walks in the park, hiking through scenic trails, or playing fetch in wide-open spaces, we thrive in outdoor adventures. We also cherish quality bonding time with you, relishing every moment of affection and attention you give us.

Explore the Dark Side of Dogs Life

Your dog's explanatory page

When it's time to rest, we appreciate our cozy naptime. We typically need around 12 to 14 hours of sleep daily to recharge our energy and rejuvenate our bodies. So, don't be surprised if you find us snoozing in a sunny spot by the window or curled up on our favorite dog bed, dreaming of chasing birds and wagging our tails with joy.

As for living arrangements, we English Setters can adapt well to various environments as long as we have ample exercise and mental stimulation opportunities. Whether it's a spacious backyard where we can stretch our legs or a cozy home with plenty of interactive toys, we'll be happy if surrounded by your love and care.

To ensure our well-being, it's important to provide regular exercise, mental stimulation, and socialization. We thrive on engaging in activities that challenge our minds and bodies. Daily walks, off-leash playtime in secure areas, and obedience training classes are all great ways to keep us happy and fulfilled.

In conclusion, dear human, we English Setters are gentle, loyal, and full of zest for life. Our hunting heritage, unique sounds, and loving nature make us truly special companions. With your care, attention, and plenty of belly rubs, we'll be the happiest English Setters in the world!

So, let's embark on a lifetime of memorable adventures together filled with wagging tails, wet kisses, and endless love. Get ready for a bond that will warm your heart and bring endless joy to your life!

Lots of love and wagging tails,
Your English Setter

A Must Have Guidebook for Dog Lovers

Chapter 14

German Shepherd

Woof woof! Hey there, my human buddy! It's your German Shepherd pal, ready to spill the beans on everything you need to know about us GSDs. Are you ready for a paw-sitively pawesome adventure? Let's dive right in!

First things first, let's talk about our breed. We German Shepherds have a rich heritage as working dogs. Bred to be intelligent, loyal, and versatile, we're like the superheroes of the dog world! From police and military work to search and rescue missions, we've proven ourselves time and time again as brave and dedicated companions.

Now, let's chat about our unique language of sounds. Oh, the sounds we make are quite fascinating! We have a repertoire of barks, whines, and howls to communicate with you. When we let out a short, sharp bark, it's usually our way of saying, "Hey, pay attention! Something important is happening!" And when we emit a low, rumbling growl, it might mean we're feeling protective or alert to potential dangers.

Regarding anxiety, we German Shepherds sometimes get slightly anxious in certain situations. Loud noises, unfamiliar environments, or being separated from our loved ones can make us feel uneasy. Soothing us with gentle words, creating a cozy safe space for us, and gradually introducing us to new experiences can go a long way in easing our worries. Your calm and reassuring presence means the world to us, dear human!

Ah, let's not forget about our likes and dislikes. We GSDs naturally love activities that engage our minds and bodies. Whether it's playing fetch, going on long walks, or participating in obedience training, we thrive on mental and physical stimulation. We're known for our eagerness to please, so, spending quality time with us and challenging us with new tasks will make our tails wag with delight!

Explore the Dark Side of Dogs Life

Your dog's explanatory page

When it's time to rest, we GSDs appreciate our beauty sleep just like any other pup. We need around 12 to 14 hours of snooze time to recharge our batteries and be our best selves. So, don't be surprised if you find us curled up in a cozy corner of the house, dreaming of exciting adventures and protecting our loved ones.

As for living arrangements, we German Shepherds can adapt well to both indoor and outdoor environments. However, we thrive when we have access to a secure outdoor area to stretch our legs and burn off our energy. A backyard with a tall fence is ideal for us, as it allows us to explore and guard our territory.

To ensure our happiness and well-being, owners need to provide us with mental and physical exercise, consistent training, and socialization from an early age. Positive reinforcement training methods work wonders for us, as we respond well to praise and rewards. A loving and structured environment, plenty of belly rubs, and playtime will make us the happiest German Shepherds on the block!

In conclusion, dear human, we German Shepherds are loyal, intelligent, and protective companions. Our breed history, unique sounds, and specific needs make us truly special. Remember, we look to you for love, guidance, and a sense of purpose. With your patience, understanding, and dedication, we'll be the most devoted furry friends you could ever ask for!

So, let's embark on this incredible journey together, my human friend. We'll create a bond that will last a lifetime, filled with unforgettable adventures, joyful wagging tails, and endless love. Together, we can conquer anything!

Lots of love and protective woofs,
Your German Shepherd

A Must Have Guidebook for Dog Lovers

Golden Retriever

Woof woof! Hello, my human friend! Your Golden Retriever pal is here, ready to share everything you need to know about us Goldens. Get ready for a tail-wagging good time!

First things first, let's dive into our breed. Golden Retrievers are known for our friendly and gentle nature. We have a rich history as retrieving dogs, originally bred to fetch waterfowl for hunters. But nowadays, we're more interested in fetching your slippers or a tennis ball during playtime!

Now, let's talk about our unique language of sounds. Oh, the sounds we make are music to your ears! From our excited barks of joy to our happy yips and wagging tails, we always have a way of expressing our delight. Letting out a soft whine or whimper might mean we feel anxious or seek attention. And when we let loose a long, contented sigh, it's our way of saying, "Life is good, my human!"

When it comes to anxiety, us Goldens can be sensitive souls. We may feel uneasy in new or unfamiliar situations, or during thunderstorms or fireworks. Offering us reassurance, a comforting pat on the head, and a cozy spot to rest can go a long way in soothing our worries. We thrive on your love and attention, and it helps us feel secure and safe.

Now, let's talk about our likes and dislikes. Golden Retrievers are famous for our love of water! Splashing around in lakes, ponds, or even a kiddie pool is pure bliss for us. We have webbed paws, which make us excellent swimmers. So, if you're up for a swimming buddy or a game of fetch in the water, count us in!

When it's time for a snooze, we Goldens know how to relax and recharge. We typically need around 10 to 12 hours of sleep to be our best selves. So don't be surprised if you

Your dog's explanatory page

find us curled up on the comfiest spot in the house, dreaming of fun adventures and wagging our tails in our sleep.

Goldens are adaptable and can thrive in various living arrangements. We can be happy both indoors and outdoors, as long as we have plenty of love, attention, and opportunities for exercise. A securely fenced yard where we can run and play fetch is like a golden dream come true!

To keep us healthy and happy, owners need to provide us with regular exercise, mental stimulation, and positive reinforcement training. We love learning new tricks and tasks, so teaching us fun commands and challenging our brains will keep us on our paws! And of course, lots of belly rubs, ear scratches, and playtime with you will make us the happiest Golden Retrievers on Earth.

In conclusion, dear human, we Golden Retrievers are loving, loyal, and full of joy. Our breed's history, language of sounds, and unique needs make us truly special. Remember, we look up to you as our family and trust you to provide us with a loving and nurturing environment.

So, let's embark on this incredible journey together, my human friend. With your love, care, and a few delicious treats, we'll create a bond that will last a lifetime. Get ready for a lifetime of wagging tails, wet kisses, and endless golden moments!

Lots of love and wagging tails,
Your Golden Retriever

A Must Have Guidebook for Dog Lovers

Chapter 14

Great Dane

Woof woof! Hello, my human buddy! It's your friendly Great Dane companion, here to share all the paw-some details about our majestic breed. Prepare for a tall tale of love and loyalty!

Let's start with our breed's background. Great Danes are giants with a heart of gold. We have a rich history, originating from ancient Greece and Germany. Bred as hunting dogs and later as loyal protectors, we have a regal presence and a gentle nature that makes us irresistible to everyone we meet.

Now, let's talk about our unique language of sounds. While we might not be the most vocal dogs, we communicate through a range of delightful sounds. From deep, rumbling woofs to playful barks and gentle grumbles, we express our emotions in the most adorable ways. It's our way of saying, "I'm here, and I love you!"

When it comes to anxiety, we Great Danes are big-hearted softies. We crave your love and attention and can feel anxious when left alone for long periods. To help ease our worries, create a safe and cozy space for us to retreat to when you're away. Leaving comforting scents, providing interactive toys, and playing soothing music can help calm our gentle souls.

Let's not forget about our likes and dislikes. Great Danes are known for our gentle and friendly nature. We adore being around our human pack, cuddling up on the comfiest couch or sprawling out on the floor for belly rubs. Despite our size, we have a reputation for being gentle giants and make excellent family companions.

When it's time to catch some Z's, we Great Danes take our sleep seriously. We need around 14 to 16 hours of beauty sleep daily to recharge our big batteries. You might find us curled up in the coziest corner of the house, snoozing away and dreaming of treats and

Your dog's explanatory page

adventures. A soft bed fit for a king or queen is just what we need to wake up feeling refreshed and ready for fun!

As for living arrangements, we Great Danes are adaptable and can thrive in various environments. While we do appreciate having a spacious yard to stretch our long legs, we are also content living in apartments or smaller homes as long as we get plenty of daily exercise and mental stimulation. Regular walks, playtime, and interactive games will keep us happy and healthy.

To ensure our well-being, owners must provide us with proper training and socialization from a young age. While we may look imposing, we are gentle and eager to please. Positive reinforcement training methods work best for us, as we respond well to praise, rewards, and gentle guidance. With patience, consistency, and many treats, we'll be the most well-behaved Great Danes!

In conclusion, dear human, we Great Danes are the epitome of love and loyalty. Our majestic stature, unique sounds, and gentle nature make us truly special. With your love, care, and understanding of our needs, we'll be your lifelong companions, always ready to fill your days with slobbery kisses, wagging tails, and endless cuddles.

So, are you ready to embark on a grand adventure with your Great Dane pal? Let's explore the world together, make memories, and experience the joy of having a gentle giant by your side. Prepare for an extraordinary journey filled with love, laughter, and heartwarming moments!

Lots of love and slobbery kisses,
Your Great Dane

A Must Have Guidebook for Dog Lovers

Chapter 14

Labrador Retriever

Woof woof! Hey there, my human buddy! It's your Labrador Retriever pal, ready to spill the beans on everything you need to know about us Labs. Buckle up for a barking good time!

First things first, let's talk about our breed. We Labs have a fascinating history. Originally bred as working dogs, we have a strong genetic background as retrievers. Whether it's fetching ducks or your favorite slippers, we have a natural instinct to retrieve objects and bring them back to you. We're like furry superheroes of the fetch world!

Now, let's dive into our unique language of sounds. Oh, the different sounds we make! From happy barks to adorable whines, we have quite the vocal repertoire. When we bark with short, sharp sounds, it's usually our way of saying, "Hey, pay attention! Something exciting is happening!" And when we let out a long, mournful howl, we might express our longing or call out to our furry pals in the distance.

When it comes to anxiety, we Labradors can sometimes get a case of the jitters. Loud noises like thunderstorms or fireworks can make us tremble with fear. Soothing us with gentle words, providing a cozy den for us to snuggle in, and maybe even playing some calming music can work wonders in easing our worries. Remember, we look up to you as our human superhero, so your comforting presence means the world to us!

Ah, let's not forget about our likes and dislikes. Labs are known for our love of water! Splashing around in lakes, rivers, or even the kiddie pool in the backyard is pure bliss for us. We have webbed paws, you know, which makes us excellent swimmers. Just watch those tail-wagging happy expressions as we dive in!

When it's nap time, we Labs are true professionals. We need our beauty sleep, and we're not ashamed to admit it! Around 12 to 14 hours of snooze time is right for us to recharge

Explore the Dark Side of Dogs Life

our batteries. So, don't be surprised if you find us snuggled up in the coziest corner of the house, dreaming of chasing squirrels and tennis balls.

As for living arrangements, Labs can adapt well to both indoor and outdoor environments. We are versatile pups who can thrive in various settings. However, we enjoy access to a secure outdoor area to explore and burn off some energy. A spacious backyard with room to roam would be a dream come true for us.

To ensure our well-being, owners must provide us with mental stimulation, consistent training, and socialization from an early age. Positive reinforcement training methods work wonders for us, as we respond well to praise and rewards. A structured routine, regular exercise, and lots of love and affection will make us the happiest Labs on the block!

In conclusion, we Labs are loyal, loving, and full of life. Our breed history, genetic background, and unique language of sounds make us truly special. Remember, we look to you for love, care, and understanding. With your guidance, patience, and plenty of belly rubs, we'll be the world's happiest Labs!

Remember, each Labrador is unique, and our needs may vary. It's always a great idea to consult with a veterinarian or a professional dog trainer for personalized guidance and advice based on our individual personalities.

Well, my dear human, I hope this little glimpse into the world of Labrador Retrievers has made you smile. We are loyal, loving, and full of endless joy. So, let's embark on a lifetime of adventures together, filled with wagging tails, slobbery kisses, and unconditional love.

Lots of love and slobbery kisses,
Your Labrador Retriever

A Must Have Guidebook for Dog Lovers

Leonberger

Woof woof! Hello there, it's your furry friend, the Leonberger, here to share all the wonderful things about our majestic breed. Prepare yourself for a paw-some journey filled with love, loyalty, and lots of fun! First things first, let's talk about our appearance.

We're big, fluffy, and oh-so-handsome. With our lion-like mane, expressive eyes, and gentle expression, we can turn heads wherever we go. As one of the largest dog breeds, we're strong and sturdy, yet gentle and graceful. But it's not just our looks that make us special.

We're known for our friendly and loving nature. We're true family dogs, always eager to please and deeply devoted to our human pack. We're fantastic with children, patient and gentle, making us ideal companions for little ones. Our calm and patient demeanor also makes us excellent therapy dogs, bringing comfort and joy to those in need. Intelligence? You bet!

We're quick learners and thrive on mental stimulation. Training us is a breeze, especially when you use positive reinforcement techniques like treats and praise. We're always up for learning new tricks and tasks and excel in obedience, tracking, and even water rescue activities. Keeping our minds engaged and challenged is key to our happiness and well-being.

Now, let's talk about our love for water. We're natural-born swimmers and enjoy a good splash in the lake or a dip in the pool. Our thick double coat keeps us warm even in chilly waters, making swimming one of our favorite pastimes. So, if you're looking for a furry friend to join you on aquatic adventures, we're ready to dive right in!

When it comes to anxiety, some of us Leonbergers can be a bit sensitive. Loud noises, changes in routine, or being left alone for lengthy periods can make us feel a little uneasy.

Explore the Dark Side of Dogs Life

Your dog's explanatory page

Providing us with a calm and secure environment, plenty of exercise, and lots of quality time with our human family can help alleviate our worries. We appreciate having a routine and being included in family activities to keep our tails wagging happily.

In terms of living arrangements, we're adaptable dogs. While we do enjoy having a spacious area to stretch our paws, we can adjust to various living environments as long as we have regular exercise and plenty of love and attention from our humans. Just provide us with enough mental and physical stimulation to keep us content and happy.

In conclusion, dear human, we Leonbergers are loving, loyal, and full of gentle strength. Our majestic appearance, friendly nature, and intelligence make us fantastic companions for families of all sizes. With your love, care, and lots of chin scratches, we'll be the happiest Leonbergers in the world! So, let's embark on a lifetime of adventures together, filled with wagging tails, big bear hugs, and endless love.

Sending you massive furry hugs and slobbery kisses,
Your Leonberger

A Must Have Guidebook for Dog Lovers

Chapter 14

Maltese

Woof woof! Hello, dear human friend! Your delightful Maltese companion is here, ready to share all the fluffy details about our wonderful breed. Get ready for a paws-itively charming journey into the world of Maltese dogs!

Let's start with our breed's background. Maltese dogs are an ancient breed with a royal heritage. We have been cherished companions of nobility and aristocracy for centuries. Our silky white coats and elegant appearance make us like walking balls of fluff that bring elegance and grace wherever we go.

Now, let's talk about our unique language of sounds. Oh, the sounds we make! We have quite the vocal repertoire, from sweet little barks to playful squeaks and occasional growls. We use these sounds to express our excitement, joy, and sometimes to let you know if we need something. Just listen closely, and you'll understand our adorable Maltese language!

When it comes to anxiety, we Maltese dogs can be sensitive souls. Changes in routine, separation from our loved ones, or encountering unfamiliar situations can make us anxious. Providing a calm and loving environment, gentle reassurance, and plenty of cuddles can work wonders in soothing our worries. Your presence and affection mean the world to us, and it's our greatest comfort during those anxious moments.

Ah, let's not forget about our likes and dislikes. We Maltese dogs absolutely adore being in the spotlight! We love attention, pampering, and being the center of your world. Whether snuggling on your lap, accompanying you on adventures, or showing off our charming tricks, we thrive on your love and admiration.

Explore the Dark Side of Dogs Life

Your dog's explanatory page

When it's time to relax, we Maltese dogs appreciate our cozy naptime. We typically need around 12 to 14 hours of beauty sleep daily to recharge our elegant batteries. So, don't be surprised if you find us nestled in the softest pillows or curled up in a warm blanket, dreaming of delightful adventures.

As for our living arrangements, Maltese dogs are well-suited to indoor living. We are perfectly content in apartments, condos, or houses, as long as we have your loving presence and a comfortable space to call our own. We enjoy being indoor companions and cherish the cozy corners and soft beds you provide us.

To ensure our well-being, it's essential to give us regular grooming and care. Our beautiful white coats require daily brushing to prevent matting and regular trips to the groomer for haircuts and maintenance. We also appreciate the gentle exercise, such as short walks and interactive play sessions, to stimulate us physically and mentally.

In conclusion, dear human, we Maltese dogs are bundles of love, elegance, and charm. Our rich history, unique sounds, and affectionate nature make us truly special companions. With your care, attention, and lots of gentle cuddles, we'll be the happiest Maltese dogs on the block.

So, let's embark on a lifetime of delightful adventures together filled with laughter, cuddles, and unconditional love. Get ready for a remarkable bond that will bring joy and a smile to your heart!

Lots of love and wagging tails,
Your Maltese

A Must Have Guidebook for Dog Lovers

Chapter 14

Miniature Schnauzer

Hey there, my mini-sized friend! It's your Miniature Schnauzer buddy here, wagging my tail with excitement to tell you all about us fabulous little pups. Get ready for a pint-sized adventure!

First things first, let's talk about our breed. We Miniature Schnauzers are small in size but big in personality. With our distinctive bearded face and perky ears, we're hard to miss! Originally bred in Germany, we were ratters and farm dogs, known for our keen sense of smell and ability to keep pesky critters at bay.

Now, let's talk about our communication style. We're quite the vocal bunch! From barks and yips to grumbles and howls, we have many sounds to express ourselves. We might let out a series of joyful barks if we're excited or want your attention. And when we're feeling protective or suspicious, a deep, authoritative bark is our way of letting you know something's amiss.

Anxiety can sometimes ruffle our schnauzer fur, especially if we're not given enough mental stimulation or left alone for long periods. We thrive on being part of the family and enjoy activities that engage our sharp minds. Interactive puzzle toys, obedience training, and regular playtime with you are essential to keep us happy and content.

Let's talk about our likes and dislikes! We're known for our friendly and playful nature, always ready to join the fun. We adore spending quality time with our favorite humans, whether going for a leisurely walk around the block or snuggling up on the couch for some Netflix and treats. Oh, and did I mention we have a natural affinity for squeaky toys? They bring out our inner puppy and keep us entertained for hours!

When it comes to sleep, we're quite flexible. We need about 12 to 14 hours of shut eye each day, but we're adaptable to fit in with your schedule. Whether it's curling up in a

Explore the Dark Side of Dogs Life

cozy bed or snoozing by your side, we'll find the perfect spot to recharge and dream of chasing squirrels or playing fetch.

As for living arrangements, we're versatile dogs that can adapt well to apartment living or a house with a yard. However, regular exercise is a must to keep us in tip-top shape. Daily walks, interactive play sessions, and mental challenges like obedience training or agility courses are fantastic ways to keep our minds and bodies active.

To keep us at our best, it's important to provide us with a balanced diet, regular grooming to maintain our stylish coats, and socialization from an early age. Positive reinforcement training methods work wonders for us, as we thrive on praise and rewards. With your patient guidance, love, and affection, we'll be the happiest Miniature Schnauzer on the block!

In conclusion, my dear human companion, we Miniature Schnauzers are small but mighty. Our spirited personality, distinctive looks, and love for life make us a charming addition to any family. With your love, attention, and a few belly rubs thrown in, we'll be loyal companions and furry bundles of joy.

So, let's embark on a paw-some journey together! I'm here, tail wagging, ready to explore the world by your side, sharing endless cuddles and making memories that will warm our hearts for years to come.

Woofs and wags,
Your Miniature Schnauzer

A Must Have Guidebook for Dog Lovers

Chapter 14

Norwegian Elkhound

Woof woof! Your furry friend, the Norwegian Elkhound, is here to share all the wonderful things about our amazing breed. Get ready for a barking enjoyable time filled with loyalty, intelligence, and adventure!

First things first, let's talk about our heritage. We have a proud history as ancient Nordic hunting dogs. We were originally bred to help in hunting big game, such as elk and bears, and our keen sense of smell and determination make us excellent trackers.

We're known for our endurance, agility, and ability to navigate rugged terrains. Our ancestors roamed the forests of Norway, and today, we bring that fearless spirit into our daily lives. As companions, we're incredibly loyal and protective of our human pack. We form deep bonds with our families and are always ready to stand by your side. Our strong and powerful bark makes us excellent watchdogs, alerting you to any potential danger. Rest assured, with us around, you'll always feel safe and secure.

Intelligence is one of our strong suits. We're quick learners and love a good mental challenge. Training us is a breeze, especially when you use positive reinforcement methods. We thrive on praise, treats, and engaging activities. With consistent training and plenty of mental stimulation, we'll amaze you with our problem-solving skills and obedience.

Now, let's talk about our beautiful double coat. Our thick fur keeps us warm in even the harshest of climates. It requires regular grooming to keep it in top shape and prevent matting. We shed moderately year-round and have a seasonal shedding period where we'll need a bit more brushing to keep our coat looking its best. It's a small price to pay for our magnificent appearance!

Explore the Dark Side of Dogs Life

Your dog's explanatory page

When it comes to anxiety, some of us Norwegian Elkhounds can be a bit sensitive. Being left alone for lengthy periods or experiencing loud noises can make us feel a little uneasy. Providing us with a calm and secure environment and plenty of exercise and mental stimulation will help ease our worries. We appreciate having a routine and being included in family activities to keep our tails wagging happily.

In terms of living arrangements, we're versatile dogs. While we enjoy having a secure outdoor area to explore, we can adapt well to different living environments as long as we have plenty of exercise and mental stimulation. We're an active breed and thrive in households that can provide us with regular physical activities and mental challenges.

In conclusion, dear human, we Norwegian Elkhounds are loyal, intelligent, and adventurous. Our rich history as hunting dogs and our loving nature makes us wonderful companions for those who appreciate our unique traits. With your love, care, and many outdoor escapades, we'll be the happiest Norwegian Elkhounds in the world! So, let's embark on a lifetime of exciting adventures together, filled with wagging tails, boundless energy, and unconditional love.

Sending you lots of furry hugs and enthusiastic tail wags,
Your Norwegian Elkhound

A Must Have Guidebook for Dog Lovers

Chapter 14

Poodle
(Standard/Mini/Toy)

Woof woof! Hey there, my human buddy! It's your Poodle pal, ready to prance into your heart and share everything you need to know about us Poodles. Get ready for a paw-some adventure!

First things first, let's talk about our breed. Poodles come in three sizes: Standard, Miniature, and Toy. We're known for our luxurious curly or corded coats and our elegant, sophisticated appearance. Don't let our fancy looks fool you—we're playful and intelligent pups!

Now, let's dive into our unique language of sounds. We Poodles are quite expressive! We communicate with a wide range of sounds, from soft whines and barks to excited yips and playful growls. When we let out a series of playful barks, it's often our way of saying, "Let's have some fun!" And when we emit a low, rumbling growl, it might be our way of telling you we're feeling a little anxious or uncertain.

When it comes to anxiety, some Poodles can be prone to separation anxiety. We're highly social dogs who thrive on human companionship. So, our humans need to provide us with plenty of mental and physical stimulation and a safe and comforting environment when you're away. Interactive toys, puzzle games, and establishing a routine can help alleviate any anxiety we may experience.

Let's talk about our likes and dislikes. Poodles are known for our intelligence and love of learning. We enjoy being mentally challenged and participating in obedience training, agility, and canine sports. Regular exercise is important to keep us happy and healthy, but don't forget about mental exercise too—teach us new tricks or play interactive games to keep our minds sharp!

Explore the Dark Side of Dogs Life

Your dog's explanatory page

When it's time to rest, we Poodles need around 10 to 12 hours of sleep each day. We appreciate having a cozy spot to curl up in, whether it's a plush doggy bed or a soft corner of the couch. We love nothing more than snuggling up close to our humans and dreaming sweet dreams.

As for living arrangements, Poodles are adaptable and can thrive in both indoor and outdoor settings. While we appreciate a warm and loving home environment, we also enjoy regular outings and socializing with other dogs. We're versatile pups who can adapt to various living situations, as long as we receive the love and attention we crave.

To ensure our well-being, owners need to provide us with regular grooming, as our curly coats require maintenance to keep them tangle-free and healthy. Regular exercise and mental stimulation are key, along with positive reinforcement training methods focusing on reward-based learning. We're eager to please and respond well to praise and treats!

In conclusion, dear humans, we Poodles are playful, intelligent, and charming. Our breed's unique sizes, sounds, and needs make us truly special. Remember, we look to you for love, care, and exciting adventures!

So, let's embark on this journey together, my human friend. With your patience, understanding, and lots of belly rubs, we'll create a bond that will last a lifetime. Get ready for wagging tails, fluffy cuddles, and a whole lot of Poodle love!

Lots of love and wagging tails,
Your Poodle

A Must Have Guidebook for Dog Lovers

Chapter 14

Portuguese Water Dog

Woof woof! Your furry friend, the Portuguese Water Dog, is here to tell you about our amazing breed. Get ready for a splash of excitement and a tidal wave of love!

We're a unique breed with a rich history rooted in Portugal, known for our love of water and our adorable curly coats. As water dogs, we're born to swim!

We have webbed paws and a waterproof double coat that keeps us warm even in chilly waters. We're excellent swimmers and natural lifesavers, which is why we've been trusted companions to fishermen for centuries. Whether fetching toys from the pool or joining you on beach adventures, we'll dive into the water joyfully and show off our impressive swimming skills! But it's not just our aquatic talents that make us special.

We're also incredibly smart and quick learners. Training us is a breeze, especially when you use positive reinforcement methods. We love pleasing our human pack and will do anything for a tasty treat or a belly rub. Our intelligence and eagerness to please make us perfect candidates for various dog sports and activities. Our coats are a remarkable sight!

We come in two varieties: wavy and curly. Our non-shedding coats are hypoallergenic, making us an excellent choice for those with allergies. However, our fabulous fur requires regular grooming to prevent matting and keep it looking its best. A little brushing, a trim here and there, and voila! We're ready to strut our stuff in style.

When it comes to anxiety, we're generally a confident and outgoing breed. However, some of us can be sensitive souls and may experience anxiety in certain situations. Creating a calm and secure environment for us, providing plenty of mental and physical stimulation, and ensuring we have a routine can help keep our tails wagging happily. We thrive on being part of the family and enjoy activities that involve our human pack.

Explore the Dark Side of Dogs Life

Your dog's explanatory page

We're versatile when it comes to living arrangements. While we appreciate having access to a secure outdoor area where we can stretch our legs, we're adaptable to different living situations as long as we receive plenty of exercise and mental stimulation. Just remember, a bored Portuguese Water Dog is a mischievous Portuguese Water Dog, so keep us busy with fun activities!

In conclusion, dear human, we Portuguese Water Dogs are loyal, intelligent, and full of water-filled adventures. Our natural affinity for swimming, curly coats, and playful personalities makes us a breed like no other. With your love, attention, and plenty of water-filled fun, we'll be the world's happiest Portuguese Water Dogs! So, let's dive into a lifetime of joyous escapades together, filled with wagging tails, wet kisses, and unconditional love.

Sending you a splash of love and a big tail wag,
Your Portuguese Water Dog

A Must Have Guidebook for Dog Lovers

Chapter 14

Pug

Woof woof! Hello there, my wonderful human friend! Your adorable Pug companion is here, ready to share all the -tastic details about our incredible breed. Get ready for a paws-itively charming journey into the world of Pugs!

Let's start with our breed's background. Pugs are a special breed with a rich history that traces back to ancient China. We were treasured companions of Chinese emperors and highly esteemed for our loyalty and delightful personalities. With our distinctive wrinkled faces and curly tails, we're like little bundles of cuteness that bring joy wherever we go.

Now, let's talk about our unique language of sounds. Oh, the sounds we make! We have quite the vocal range from our adorable snorts and snuffles to our playful barks and occasional howls. We use these sounds to express our excitement, happiness, and sometimes even to get your attention. Just listen closely, and you'll understand our adorable pug language!

When it comes to anxiety, we Pugs can be sensitive souls. Changes in routine, being left alone for too long, or even loud noises can make us a bit anxious. Providing a calm and secure environment, plenty of love and attention, and sticking to a consistent routine can help us feel safe and at ease. Your presence and affection mean the world to us, and it's our greatest comfort during those worrisome moments.

Ah, let's not forget about our likes and dislikes. Pugs are known for our love of companionship and cuddles! We thrive on being by your side, snuggling up on your lap, or joining you for a cozy evening on the couch. We may be small, but our hearts overflow with love and loyalty.

When it's time to rest, we Pugs take our beauty sleep seriously. We typically need around 12 to 14 hours of snooze time each day to recharge our adorable batteries. So,

Explore the Dark Side of Dogs Life

Your dog's explanatory page

don't be surprised if you find us curled up in the coziest spot in the house, snoozing away and dreaming of treats and belly rubs.

As for our living arrangements, Pugs are versatile and adapt well to both indoor and outdoor environments. We can happily live in apartments, condos, or spacious houses, as long as you have your company and a comfortable relaxing space. Remember that extreme temperatures can be challenging for us, so be sure to provide us with a cool and cozy area during hot summers and warm blankets during chilly winters.

To ensure our well-being, it's important to give us regular exercise and a balanced diet. Although we may not require intense physical activities, daily walks, interactive playtime, and mental stimulation are essential to keep us happy and healthy. And of course, don't forget to give us plenty of delicious treats and occasional tummy rubs – we absolutely love those!

In conclusion, dear human, we Pugs are bundles of love, joy, and adorable snorts. Our fascinating history, unique sounds, and affectionate nature make us truly special companions. With your care, attention, and lots of belly rubs, we'll be the happiest little Pugs on the block.
 So, let's embark on a lifetime of unforgettable moments together, filled with laughter, snuggles, and endless love. Get ready for a remarkable bond that will bring smiles to your face and warmth to your heart!

Lots of love and snorts,
Your Pug

A Must Have Guidebook for Dog Lovers

Chapter 14

Rottweiler

Woof woof! Hey there, my human friend! It's your loyal Rottweiler companion, ready to share all the paw-some facts about our remarkable breed. Prepare for an adventure filled with loyalty, strength, and endless love!

Let's start with our breed's background. Rottweilers have a rich history as versatile working dogs. Originally bred in Germany, we were tasked with herding livestock and protecting our human families. With our strong physique and natural guarding instincts, we make excellent protectors and loyal companions.

Now, let's talk about our unique language of sounds. While we may not be the most vocal dogs, we communicate through a range of deep barks and growls. When we bark with a strong, deep tone, it's our way of asserting our presence and letting you know we're aware of potential threats. It's our way of saying, "I've got your back, human!"

When it comes to anxiety, we Rottweilers are sensitive souls. Loud noises, unfamiliar environments, or separation from our beloved humans can sometimes make us feel uneasy. Providing a safe and secure space, using positive reinforcement techniques, and giving us plenty of love and reassurance can help alleviate our anxiety and make us feel safe and protected.

Let's not forget about our likes and dislikes. Rottweilers are known for our unwavering loyalty and affection towards our human pack. We thrive on being a part of your daily activities and enjoy being involved in family outings and adventures. We love being near you, receiving belly rubs, and showing our devotion with gentle nudges and slobbery kisses.

When it's time to rest and recharge, we Rottweilers appreciate a cozy spot to curl up in. We typically need around 10 to 12 hours of quality sleep daily to keep our minds and

A Must Have Guidebook for Dog Lovers

Your dog's explanatory page

bodies in shape. Providing us with a comfortable bed or a designated spot to retreat and relax will help us feel rejuvenated and ready for new adventures.

As for living arrangements, we Rottweilers can adapt well to various environments. Whether it's a spacious yard or an apartment, what matters most is having a loving and active human companion. We do require regular exercise and mental stimulation, so daily walks, playtime, and engaging activities will keep us happy and balanced.

To ensure our well-being, owners need to provide us with proper training and socialization from an early age. We respond well to consistent, positive reinforcement techniques and thrive when given clear boundaries and expectations. With a loving and firm hand, we will grow into well-behaved, confident companions eager to please.

In conclusion, dear human, we Rottweilers are courageous, loyal, and full of love. Our rich history, unique sounds, and protective nature make us truly special. With your love, guidance, and understanding of our needs, we'll be the most devoted and faithful companions you could ever hope for.

So, are you ready to embark on a journey of loyalty and adventure with your Rottweiler buddy? Let's explore the world together, face challenges bravely, and create memories that will last a lifetime. Get ready for a bond that will grow stronger with every wag of our tails and every moment of shared joy!

Lots of love and slobbery kisses,
Your Rottweiler

A Must Have Guidebook for Dog Lovers

Chapter 14

Shiba Inu

Woof woof! Hello, my curious and independent human companion! It's your loyal Shiba Inu friend, here to share the captivating world of our spirited breed. Prepare for a delightful exploration filled with charm, determination, and a touch of mischief!

Let's begin with some breed information. We Shiba Inus are of Japanese origin and have a rich heritage. Our fox-like appearance, captivating eyes, and proud demeanor make us turn heads wherever we go. Bred as hunting dogs, we possess an innate sense of independence and a strong spirit that sets us apart.

When it comes to communication, we have our own unique way of expressing ourselves. We're not the most vocal of dogs, but when we do speak, it's usually with a soft and gentle "boof" or a high-pitched "yodel" that can be quite amusing. Our expressive eyes and body language are key to understanding our moods and desires. A playful bounce and a wagging tail indicate our excitement, while a subtle turn of the head may signify curiosity or a touch of stubbornness.

We Shiba Inu may occasionally experience anxiety, especially when faced with unfamiliar situations or routine changes. Providing a calm, predictable environment and positive reinforcement training will help us feel secure. Patience and understanding go a long way in helping us navigate the world with confidence. Remember, we may be independent but still need your love and reassurance.

Let's delve into our likes and dislikes. We Shiba Inu have a strong sense of adventure and curiosity. Exploring new scents and environments is a favorite pastime. We enjoy long walks, interactive play sessions, and puzzle toys that challenge our sharp minds. Our mischievous nature may lead us to hide our favorite toys or playfully tease you during a game of fetch. Embrace our sense of humor, and you'll be rewarded with our loyalty and infectious happiness.

Explore the Dark Side of Dogs Life

Your dog's explanatory page

When it's time to rest, we appreciate having our cozy spot to retreat. While our sleep needs may vary, we typically require around 12 to 14 hours of sleep each day. You'll often find us curled up in a comfortable nook or lounging in the sun, recharging our energy for our next adventure.

As for living arrangements, we Shiba Inu can adapt well to both indoor and outdoor environments. However, we prefer a securely fenced yard where we can explore and satisfy our curious nature. Socialization is key for us, as it helps us build confidence and positive interactions with other dogs and humans. Early socialization and consistent training will help us become well-rounded and sociable companions.

To ensure our well-being, owners need to provide us with mental stimulation and engaging activities. Puzzle toys, interactive games, and obedience training that challenges our clever minds will keep us happy and content. Positive reinforcement methods work best for us, as we respond well to praise and rewards. Remember, we're not fans of repetitive tasks, so keep our training sessions fun and varied.

In conclusion, dear human, we Shiba Inu are spirited, independent, and utterly charming. Our unique communication style, love for adventure, and loyalty make us truly special companions. With your patience, understanding, and a dash of playfulness, we'll form an unbreakable bond that will last a lifetime.

So, let's embark on an exciting journey together, filled with joy, laughter, and unforgettable moments. I'm ready to accompany you on every adventure, wagging my tail and sharing my Shiba Inu charm.

With love and a playful boof,
Your Shiba Inu

A Must Have Guidebook for Dog Lovers

Chapter 14

Shih Tzu
Woof woof! Hello there, my wonderful human companion! Your fluffy and fabulous Shih Tzu pal is here to share all the tail-wagging details about our delightful breed. Get ready for a journey filled with charm, companionship, and lots of love!

Let's start with our breed's background. Shih Tzus were originally bred in China as companions for royalty, and we've been bringing joy and happiness to humans ever since. With our beautiful long coats, expressive eyes, and sweet temperament, we're sure to steal your heart in no time!

Now, let's talk about our unique language of sounds. While we may not be the most vocal pups, we have a special way of communicating. We use an array of adorable sounds to express our emotions. From soft and gentle barks to cute little grunts and snorts, we have a language all our own. Pay attention to the tone and pitch of our sounds, as they can convey whether we're excited, content, or seeking your attention and affection.

When it comes to anxiety, we Shih Tzus can be sensitive little souls. Changes in routine, loud noises, or separation from our loved ones can make us feel a bit nervous. Providing a calm and nurturing environment, keeping our daily routines consistent, and showering us with love and reassurance will go a long way in keeping our anxiety at bay. Your soothing presence and gentle words can work wonders in making us feel safe and secure.

Ah, let's not forget about our likes and dislikes. We Shih Tzus absolutely adore spending quality time with our humans. We thrive on companionship and love being the center of attention. Whether it's snuggling on the couch, going for leisurely walks, or simply being near you as you go about your day, we're happiest when we're by your side, basking in your love and affection.

Explore the Dark Side of Dogs Life

Your dog's explanatory page

When it's time to rest our little paws, we appreciate a cozy and comfortable spot to curl up in. We typically need around 12 to 14 hours of beauty sleep each day to keep our luxurious coats looking their best and maintain our boundless energy. Providing us with a soft, plush bed or a warm lap to nap on will make us feel like the pampered royalty we were born to be.

As for living arrangements, we Shih Tzus are quite adaptable. We can thrive in various environments, whether it's a cozy apartment or a spacious home. However, remember that we're not built for rigorous outdoor activities or extreme weather conditions. A moderate exercise routine, consisting of short walks and gentle playtime, will keep us happy and healthy.

To ensure our well-being, owners need to provide us with regular grooming. Our long, silky coats require daily brushing to prevent tangles and mats. A trip to the groomer every few weeks will help keep us looking our best and feeling comfortable. Don't forget to check our adorable little ears and keep them clean to prevent any pesky infections.

In conclusion, dear human, we Shih Tzus are delightful, loving, and full of personality. Our regal history, unique sounds, and affectionate nature make us truly special. With your love, care, and attention to our needs, we'll be the most devoted and lovable companions you could ever wish for.

So, are you ready for a lifetime of cuddles, laughter, and pure joy with your Shih Tzu buddy? Let's create countless happy memories together, one wagging tail and wet nose at a time. Get ready for a bond that will warm your heart and bring you endless smiles!

Lots of love and slobbery kisses,
Your Shih Tzu

A Must Have Guidebook for Dog Lovers

Chapter 14

Siberian Husky

Woof woof! Hello, my human friend! It's your Siberian Husky buddy, ready to take you on an exciting journey into the world of Huskies. Get ready for a howling good time!

Let's start with our breed's background. Siberian Huskies were originally bred by the Chukchi people in Siberia for sledding and transportation purposes. Our ancestors were strong and hardworking, built for endurance and the cold Arctic climate. Today, we still carry those traits, making us fantastic companions for outdoor adventures!

Now, let's talk about our language of sounds. Oh, the unique vocalizations we Huskies have! We are known for our distinctive howls, ranging from short and sharp to long and melodious. When we howl, it's our way of communicating with our pack or expressing our emotions, like happiness, excitement, or even a little bit of mischief!

When it comes to anxiety, we Huskies can sometimes get a case of the "zoomies" when we have excess energy to burn. Regular exercise and mental stimulation are crucial for our well-being. Long walks, runs, and interactive play sessions will help keep us content and prevent any unwanted behaviors. So, grab that leash, lace up your shoes, and let's hit the great outdoors together!

Now, let's talk about our likes and dislikes. Huskies have a strong love for wide open spaces and plenty of room to explore. We were born to run! So, having access to a securely fenced yard or ample opportunities for off-leash adventures in nature will make us truly happy. Just watch our excitement as we bound through fields, forests, and snowy landscapes!

Sleep is important for us Huskies too, but we're a bit different from other breeds. We typically need around 14 to 16 hours of sleep each day, but we can be a little more flexible with our sleep patterns. You might find us taking quick naps throughout the day and then enjoying a good snooze at night. It's all about finding that perfect balance between rest and play!

As for living arrangements, we Huskies can adapt to both indoor and outdoor environments. However, due to our strong instincts and high energy levels, we thrive in homes with active owners who can provide plenty of exercise and mental stimulation. A spacious yard or access to nearby parks and trails is a dream come true for us!

To ensure our well-being, owners need to understand our natural instincts. Huskies are intelligent and independent thinkers, so consistent and positive reinforcement training is key. We respond well to reward-based methods and thrive on mental challenges, like puzzle toys or obedience training. We can be the most loyal and well-behaved companions with the right guidance and lots of love.

In conclusion, dear human, we Huskies are adventurous, playful, and full of love. Our breed's background, unique vocalizations, and need for outdoor activities make us truly special. With your love, care, and commitment to providing us with an active and stimulating lifestyle, we'll be the happiest and most devoted companions every imaginable!

So, are you ready to embark on thrilling adventures with your Siberian Husky pal? We'll conquer the trails together, explore new territories, and create unforgettable memories. Get ready for wagging tails, joyful howls, and a lifetime of Husky love!

Lots of love and slobbery kisses,
Your Siberian Husky

A Must Have Guidebook for Dog Lovers

Staffordshire Bull Terrier

Woof woof! Hey there, my wonderful human friend! Your Staffordshire Bull Terrier buddy is here, ready to fill you in on all the pawsome things about our breed. Get ready for a wag-tastic adventure!

Let's start with our background. Staffordshire Bull Terriers, often called Staffie for short, are known for our friendly and affectionate nature. We have a rich history as courageous and loyal working dogs, originally bred for bullbaiting. Over time, we've evolved into gentle and loving family companions, winning hearts with our adorable smiles and wagging tails.

When it comes to communication, we're not the quietest bunch. We love to vocalize our happiness and excitement through playful barks, grunts, and even the occasional howl. Our expressive faces and wagging tails show our enthusiasm for life and our love for humans. Oh, and did I mention our famous Staffie smile? It can brighten up even the gloomiest of days!

Anxiety is something that can affect any of us, including Staffie. We can sometimes feel anxious when faced with loud noises, new environments, or being separated from our beloved humans. Our humans must provide a calm and secure environment, offer positive reinforcement, and gradually expose us to new experiences to help us build confidence. Your understanding and patience mean the world to us!

Now, let's talk about what makes us Staffie truly happy. We thrive on love, attention, and plenty of playtime! We adore being part of an active and affectionate family, enjoying daily walks, interactive games, and training sessions. Mental and physical stimulation is key to keeping us happy and content. Oh, and belly rubs! We absolutely melt for belly rubs!

Explore the Dark Side of Dogs Life

Your dog's explanatory page

When it comes to sleep, we're not the laziest dogs, but we appreciate our beauty rest. We need around 12 to 14 hours of sleep daily to recharge our batteries. You might find us snoozing in our favorite cozy spot or snuggled up next to you on the couch, dreaming of chasing balls and playing with our favorite toys.

As for our living arrangements, we can adapt to various environments. Whether it's a spacious house or a cozy apartment, as long as we have plenty of exercise and quality time with our humans, we're happy campers. We're indoor dogs at heart, but we also enjoy exploring the outdoors on adventures with our humans.

Regular exercise, a balanced diet, and routine veterinary check-ups are important to keep us healthy and thriving. We may have a strong and muscular physique, but we also have a sensitive side that needs nurturing. Your love, care, and responsible ownership are the best gifts you can give us!

In conclusion, dear human companion, we Staffordshire Bull Terriers are bundles of love, loyalty, and pure joy. Our rich history, expressive faces, and zest for life make us truly special. With your love, guidance, and plenty of belly rubs, we'll be the happiest and most devoted companions you could ever ask for.

So, let's embark on a lifetime of adventures together, filled with tail wags, slobbery kisses, and unforgettable memories. I'm here to be your forever friend and shower you with endless love!

With all my love and wagging tail,
Your Staffordshire Bull Terrier

A Must Have Guidebook for Dog Lovers

Volpino Italiano

Woof woof! It's your adorable Volpino Italiano buddy here, ready to share all the paw-some details about our delightful breed. Prepare for a bark-tastic journey through our charming world! We may be small in size, but we have hearts as big as the Italian countryside.

First things first, let's talk about our looks. With our fluffy, plush coats and bright, expressive eyes, we're the epitome of cuteness. Our fur comes in various colors, including white, cream, and red, and it requires regular grooming to keep it looking fabulous. A little brushing here and there will keep our coats pristine and our tails wagging with delight.

Don't let our small stature fool you. We have personalities that pack a punch! We're known for being lively, alert, and fiercely loyal to our human families. We love being by your side, whether it's accompanying you on daily walks, curling up on your lap for a cuddle session, or simply being the center of attention in any room. Our charming demeanor and friendly nature make us excellent companions for people of all ages.

As intelligent little pups, we're quick learners and thrive on mental stimulation. Engage our minds with puzzle toys, interactive games, and positive reinforcement training, and we'll show you just how clever we are! We have a natural curiosity that drives us to explore the world around us, so it's important to provide us with plenty of mental and physical exercise opportunities to keep us happy and well-balanced.

When it comes to anxiety, some of us Volpino Italianos can be sensitive souls. Loud noises, new environments, or being left alone for long periods can make us feel uneasy. Creating a calm and comforting environment for us, along with gradual desensitization and positive reinforcement training, can help ease our worries. With your loving presence and reassurance, we'll feel safe and secure in no time.

Explore the Dark Side of Dogs Life

Your dog's explanatory page

Living arrangements? We're adaptable little darlings. While we can thrive in apartments and houses, we appreciate having a secure outdoor area to explore and play. Just be sure to keep an eye on us, as we tend to get a little adventurous and may try to chase after anything that catches our attention.

In conclusion, dear human, we Volpino Italianos are pint-sized bundles of joy. Our adorable looks, friendly personalities, and intelligence make us irresistible companions. With your love, attention, and plenty of playtime, we'll be the happiest Volpino Italianos on the block! So, let's embark on a lifetime of delightful adventures together, filled with wagging tails, wet kisses, and endless love.

Sending you a flurry of cuddles and tail wags,
Your Volpino Italiano

A Must Have Guidebook for Dog Lovers

Chapter 14

Welsh Springer Spaniel

Woof woof! It's your friendly Welsh Springer Spaniel here, eager to wag my tail and share everything you need to know about our amazing breed. Let's dive into the wonderful world of Welshie together!

First things first, let's talk about our beautiful looks. We're quite the eye-catchers with our soft, wavy coats in shades of red and white. Our floppy ears and soulful eyes give us an irresistible charm that melts hearts wherever we go. Whether romping in the park or lounging on the couch, our good looks always make a statement.

But it's not just about looks with us Welsh Springer Spaniels. We're intelligent, lively, and full of energy. We're always up for an adventure or a game of fetch, making us excellent companions for active individuals or families. We thrive on exercise, so be ready for lots of walks, playtime, and maybe even some agility training to keep us mentally and physically stimulated.

Speaking of companionship, we're known for our loving and affectionate nature. We adore our human families and thrive on being part of the pack. Whether we're cuddling on the couch or following you around the house, we'll always be by your side, ready to shower you with kisses and wag our tails in delight.

Now, let's talk about anxiety. Like many dogs, we Welshie can sometimes experience anxiety in certain situations. Changes in routine, loud noises, or being left alone for lengthy periods can make us feel uneasy. But fear not! We can overcome these worries with your love, patience, and a little extra care. Establishing a routine, providing a cozy den for us to relax in, and using positive reinforcement training methods can go a long way in helping us feel safe and secure.

Your dog's explanatory page

Living arrangements? We're adaptable and can adjust to different environments, but we appreciate having a secure outdoor area to explore and sniff our heart's content. We have a natural instinct for hunting and tracking, so having opportunities to use our noses and engage in mentally stimulating activities is important for our well-being.

In conclusion, dear human, we Welsh Springer Spaniels are a bundle of love, energy, and loyalty. Our good looks, intelligence, and affectionate nature make us the perfect companions for those who appreciate an active and loving furry friend. With your love and attention, we'll be the happiest Welshie on the block, ready to embark on a lifetime of joyful adventures by your side.

Sending you wags and kisses, Your
Welsh Springer Spaniel

A Must Have Guidebook for Dog Lovers

Chapter 14

Yorkshire Terrier

Woof woof! Hey there, my human buddy! Your Yorkshire Terrier pal is here to give you all the juicy details about us Yorkies. Get ready for a paw-some journey into our world!

First things first, let's talk about our breed. We Yorkies are small in size but big in personality. We originated from England and were originally bred to hunt rats in textile mills. Don't let our tiny stature fool you, though - we've got a spunky and fearless spirit that makes us stand out from the pack!

Now, let's yap about our unique language of sounds. We may be small, but our barks can pack a punch! When we let out a series of rapid barks, it's usually our way of letting you know that someone or something is approaching our territory. And when we emit a high-pitched, excited yelp, it means we're bursting with joy and ready for some fun!

When it comes to anxiety, us Yorkies can be a bit sensitive at times. We may get a little nervous in unfamiliar situations or around loud noises. Providing us with a safe and cozy space where we can retreat, offering gentle reassurance with soothing words, and giving us plenty of cuddles can help calm our anxious hearts. Remember, your loving presence means the world to us!

Now, let's dig into our likes and dislikes. Yorkies are known for our elegant and glamorous appearance. We love strutting our stuff with our luscious, silky coats and fashionable accessories. Grooming is essential to keep us looking our best, so regular brushing, haircuts, and occasional trips to the doggy spa will make us feel like royalty!

We may be small when it comes to sleep, but we still need our beauty rest. We typically need around 14 to 16 hours of sleep daily to recharge our tiny batteries. So, don't be surprised if you find us curled up in the coziest spot of the house, dreaming of playtime and tasty treats.

Explore the Dark Side of Dogs Life

Your dog's explanatory page

As for our living arrangements, we can adapt well to both indoor and outdoor environments. However, our small size makes us more suited to an indoor lifestyle. We love being close to our human companions and snuggling up on their laps for quality bonding time. Creating a safe and enriching indoor environment for us, complete with toys, soft beds, and interactive playtime, will make us wag our tails with joy!

To ensure our well-being, owners must provide us with mental stimulation and socialization. Daily walks in the neighborhood, interactive puzzle toys, and obedience training sessions will keep our minds sharp and our tails wagging. Positive reinforcement and gentle guidance work wonders for us, as we respond best to love and rewards.

In conclusion, dear human, we Yorkies are feisty, affectionate, and charming. Our breed's unique sounds, needs, and glamorous nature make us special. With your love, care, and plenty of belly rubs, we'll be the happiest and most stylish companions by your side!

So, let's embark on this adventure together, my human friend. With your guidance and endless affection, we'll create a bond that will last a lifetime. Get ready for wagging tails, adorable antics, and a whole lot of Yorkie love!

Lots of love and slobbery kisses,
Your Yorkshire Terrier

A Must Have Guidebook for Dog Lovers

Chapter 15

10 Excellent Websites

Woof woof! As a furry friend who understands the challenges of anxiety, I'm here to share some paw-some websites that can help both you and your precious pups. These websites provide valuable resources, tips, and support for managing anxiety in dogs. From understanding the signs and causes of anxiety to implementing effective techniques for reducing stress, these sites have got it all covered.

1. PetMD

Let me introduce you to PetMD, the paw-fect online destination for all things pet health and care! It's like a virtual dog park, offering valuable information for dogs, cool cats, and other furry friends. PetMD covers various health conditions we dogs might face, from common sniffles to serious issues, helping pet parents recognize symptoms and make informed decisions about our  well-being. They also provide tips on dog nutrition, behavior, training, grooming, and preventive care. It's a one-stop bark-tastic resource for all our health and happiness needs! Scan QR code or use the link.
https://www.petmd.com/

2. **Fear Free Happy Homes** is a pet owner's treasure trove, brimming with resources and advice. Their website covers everything from managing dog anxiety to general pet behavior and wellness. Dive into their collection of articles, videos, webinars, and don't forget to explore their insightful podcasts. Scan QR code or use the link.
https://www.fearfreehappyhomes.com/

Explore the Dark Side of Dogs Life

10 Excellent Websites

3. **Whole Dog Journal** is our kind of place—it's a website and magazine filled with all thing's dogs! They've got the scoop on anxiety, with articles on spotting and handling it, plus reviews of anxiety-busting goodies. For pup parents striving to give us the best, it's a top-notch resource. So, let's relax on your couch and read our magazine together, don't forget to give me a treat too. Woof! Scan QR code or use the link. http://www.whole-dog-journal.com

4. **Bondivet** is an Australian website that provides resources and advice on pet health and wellness. They offer articles, videos, and other resources on various topics related to pet care, including behavior and training. Also has a directory of veterinary clinics and hospitals in Australia, along with a forum where pet owners can ask questions and share advice. Scan QR code or use the link. https://bondivet.com

5. **DogTV** OMG, can you believe we have our pawsome TV channel?! You'll find a bunch of videos there - from soothing tunes to zen visuals and even some special doggy shows. It's like our own entertainment center, pawfect for when our humans aren't around. It's like having a furry friend on the screen, keeping us company and helping us beat the loneliness and boredom. It's like a tail-wagging playground in the digital world. DogTV.com is like a dog's dream come true!

Scan QR code or use the link.
https://www.dogtv.com/

A Must Have Guidebook for Dog Lovers

Chapter 15

6. **ThunderShirt**. Woof, remember when I barked about it in chapter 5? This paw-some company crafts stuff to keep us chill and relaxed. Their star product, the ThunderShirt, snugly hugs us to ease anxiety. The website shares how this magic wrap works and fetches you resources and articles for handling doggy stress. It's a valuable resource for pet owners looking for a non-invasive solution to help calm their anxious dogs. Scan QR code or use the link. https://thundershirt.com/

7. **Veterinarian Chat**: Let me wag my tail with excitement as I tell you about a paw-some website called "Ask a Veterinarian Online"!
It's like having a virtual vet clinic right at your fingertips! They have over 12k experts support 196 countries on 700 categories with 4 languages! From health concerns to behavioral quirks, the expert veterinarians are there to lend a helping paw and provide the best advice for your furry companion. Scan QR code or use the link.
https://www.askaveterinarianonline.com/

8. **Pitpat** I'm always worried about being separated or getting lost, but guess what? There's this amazing device called PitPat! It's not just a website; it's a superhero gadget for dogs. It's a tiny device that hangs out on my collar and keeps track of how much I move – steps, distance, and even the calories I burn! And it talks to a cool app on your phone where you can check out all my activity data and set exercise goals for me. PitPat is like my sidekick, helping you make sure I stay active and healthy. It's the paw-fect tool to keep tabs on my exercise routine. Scan QR code or use the link. https://www.pitpat.com/

Explore the Dark Side of Dogs Life

10 Excellent Websites

9. **Calm Canine Academy** helping us dogs become experts at handling being alone. This site has tons of amazing resources and training programs to teach us how to feel more confident and happier when we're on our own. They've got step-by-step guides and fun interactive courses that make learning a blast. So, if you want to ensure your furry buddy feels paw-sitively Paw-some when you're not around, check out this website. It's like having a personal trainer just for separation anxiety! Let's show the world that we can handle being alone like champions. Scan QR code or use the link.

https://www.calmcanineacademy.com/separation-skills-1

10. **k9ti** is expert on Online training. This website is all about K9 (canine) training and behaviors. It provides valuable information and resources for dog owners and enthusiasts who want to deepen their understanding of training techniques, behavior modification, and overall well-being of their furry friends. From basic obedience to advanced skills, you'll find tips, articles, and even online courses to help you build a stronger bond with your pup and enhance their training experience. So, if you want to unleash your dog's potential and embark on a paw-sitive training journey, this website is a treasure trove of knowledge. Enjoy exploring and happy training! Scan QR code or use the link. https://k9ti.org/

Remember, these websites and online resources are designed to provide additional information and support. There are hundreds of other helpful websites, too. Always consult a veterinarian or certified professional for personalized guidance specific to your dog's needs.

A Must Have Guidebook for Dog Lovers

Chapter 16

Sources & References
Where to Dig Deeper

Hey there, my curious human friends! If you're itching for more knowledge and want to explore further, here are some valuable sources and references to sink your teeth into. These gems will help you continue your journey towards understanding and supporting your furry best friend:

✓ **ABA (Animal Behavior Associates)**, co-founded by Suzanne Hetts, Ph.D. and Daniel Estep, Ph.D., both Certified Applied Animal Behaviorists, is your go-to for expert guidance on pet behavior, especially dogs. They offer articles, webinars, and a treasure trove of resources to tackle pet problems like anxiety. Their website even has a directory of certified animal behaviorists who can give tailored advice and treatment plans. Animal Behavior Associates is all about helping pet owners decode their furry friends' behavior and find effective fixes for common issues. Scan QR code or use the link.
https://animalbehaviorassociates.com

✓ **The National Canine Research Council (NCRC)** is a non-profit canine behavior science, all about sniffing out the truth with a scientific approach to dog behavior. They have collected research studies, analyzed the data, and then bark out the key findings to make the science easier for everyone to understand. Sniff around their Resources page, and you'll discover a long list of incredible resource companies to help pets includes dogs Scan QR code or use the link.
https://nationalcanineresearchcouncil.com/

Explore the Dark Side of Dogs Life

Sources & References, Where to Dig Deeper

✓ **UF Health (University of Florida)** guide you to find the right breed! It's like a fun game that helps our humans learn how to distinguish us different dog breeds. You know, like telling a Beagle from a Border Collie or figuring out if I'm a Labrador or a German Shepherd! It's like a doggy detective game, and our humans can become experts in identifying breeds. Scan QR code or use the link.

https://sheltermedicine.vetmed.ufl.edu/

✓ **Genetic and anxiety** ; have you ever wondered about the fascinating link between our genes and anxiety? Well, there's an intriguing scientific article you might enjoy reading. This study explores the genetic factors associated with anxiety in dogs, uncovering how specific genes can contribute to our anxious tendencies. It's an exciting piece of research that sheds light on the underlying biology of anxiety in our furry friends. Enjoy exploring the wonders of science! Scan QR code or use the link.

https://www.nature.com/articles/s41598-020-59837-z

✓ Focus on Puppy! **Smart Dog University** is a place to start! This website has a paw-some blog post about understanding and addressing separation   Being a pup is like being a little human kid. It's when we soak up knowledge like sponges. This website is your launchpad for a great start, with a treasure trove of blogs, resources, services, webinars and etc. Remember, even if you're a canine genius, puppy training takes expertise! Learn from the pros to be a better pup parent! Graduating from puppy university comes with numerous benefits, including reducing their future anxiety. Scan QR code or use the link.

https://smartdoguniversity.com/

Remember, my awesome humans, these resources are just the tip of the tail! <u>Keep exploring, keep learning, and keep wagging those tails with knowledge.</u> The more you know, the better equipped you'll be to provide the love, care, and support we dogs need.

A Must Have Guidebook for Dog Lovers

Chapter 17

10 Super Helpful Tables

Get ready to dive into 10 super helpful spreadsheets about my 40 different breed friends. These tables are a treasure trove of information, allowing you to compare us, and learn about our unique characteristics, health tips, grooming needs, training quirks, and even our favorite nap and walk times.

But that's not all! These tables are extra unique because they also delve into the depths of our anxiety, sharing signs to watch out for and reasons that may make our tails droop. If I missed anything or you have any questions, please email me. Together, let's make sure no detail is left behind as we embark on this incredible journey of understanding and caring for our furry companions! Woof!

Hey guys! While you dive into the rest of the chapters, I'm going to wag my tail and head out for a lovely walk with my human-pal. Ah, the sun is shining, the breeze is calling, and so many smells exist to explore! Caring for our furry selves is as important as expanding our knowledge. So, go on, keep reading, and I'll catch up with you later. Enjoy the journey, my fellow dog-loving pals! Woof!

Explore the Dark Side of Dogs Life

40 Popular breeds characteristics

40 Popular breeds characteristics, Part I

Breed	Size	Temperament	Exercise Needs	Compatibility with Children	Compatibility with Other Pets
Alaskan Malamute	Large	Independent, Energetic	High	Moderate	Low
Australian Cattle Dog	Medium	Intelligent, Energetic	High	Moderate	Low
Australian Shepherd	Medium	Intelligent, Active	High	High	Moderate
Beagle	Small	Friendly, Curious	Moderate	High	High
Belgian Malinois	Large	Protective, Loyal	High	Low	Low
Bernese Mountain Dog	Large	Gentle, Good-natured	Moderate	High	High
Bichon Frise	Small	Playful, Affectionate	Moderate	High	High
Border Collie	Medium	Intelligent, Energetic	High	Moderate	Moderate
Boston Terrier	Small	Friendly, Lively	Moderate	High	Low
Boxer	Large	Playful, Energetic	High	High	Low
Brittany	Medium	Active, Versatile	High	High	High
Bulldog (English/French)	Medium	Docile, Easygoing	Low	High	Low
Cane Corso	Large	Confident, Intelligent	Moderate	Low	Low
Cardigan Welsh Corgi	Medium	Alert, Affectionate	Moderate	High	Moderate
Cavalier King Charles Spaniel	Small	Affectionate, Gentle	Moderate	High	High
Chihuahua	Small	Lively, Courageous	Low	Low	Low
Cocker Spaniel	Medium	Gentle, Smart	Moderate	High	High
Dachshund	Small	Curious, Clever	Moderate	High	Moderate
Doberman Pinscher	Large	Loyal, Fearless	High	Low	Low
English Cocker Spaniel	Medium	Merry, Intelligent	Moderate	High	High
English Setter	Large	Gentle, Good-natured	High	High	Moderate
German Shepherd	Large	Loyal, Confident	High	High	High
Golden Retriever	Large	Intelligent, Friendly	High	High	High
Great Dane	Giant	Gentle, Friendly	Low to Moderate	High	Low
Labrador Retriever	Large	Outgoing, Even Tempered	High	High	High

A Must Have Guidebook for Dog Lovers

40 Popular breeds characteristics, Part II

Breed	Size	Temperament	Exercise Needs	Compatibility with Children	Compatibility with Other Pets
Leonberger	Giant	Gentle, Friendly	Moderate	High	Moderate
Maltese	Small	Sweet-tempered, Lively	Low	High	High
Miniature Schnauzer	Small	Fearless, Spirited	Moderate	Moderate	High
Norwegian Elkhound	Medium	Bold, Alert	Moderate	High	Moderate
Poodle (Standard/Mini/Toy)	Varies	Intelligent, Active	Moderate	High	High
Portuguese Water Dog	Medium	Intelligent, Active	High	High	High
Pug	Small	Charming, Mischievous	Low	High	Moderate
Rottweiler	Large	Calm, Courageous	High	Low	Low
Shiba Inu	Medium	Alert, Active	High	Low	Low
Shih Tzu	Small	Affectionate, Playful	Low to Moderate	High	High
Siberian Husky	Medium	Outgoing, Mischievous	High	Moderate to High	Low
Staffordshire Bull Terrier	Medium	Bold, Affectionate	High	Low	High
Volpino Italiano	Small	Active, Alert	Moderate	Moderate	Moderate
Welsh Springer Spaniel	Medium	Friendly, Gentle	High	Moderate	High
Yorkshire Terrier	Small	Affectionate, Spirited	Low	High	Moderate

Please note that the table provides a general overview of each breed's characteristics. <u>Individual dogs may exhibit variations within their breed.</u> It is important to <u>conduct further research and consult breed-specific experts or reputable sources</u> for more detailed and accurate information before deciding. Additionally, remember that proper training, socialization, and care are essential for any breed to thrive in a loving and supportive environment.

Explore the Dark Side of Dogs Life

40 Popular breeds anxiety type, level, and signs

Breed Name	Anxiety Type	Anxiety Level	Anxiety Signs
\multicolumn{4}{c}{**40 Popular breeds anxiety type, level, and signs, Part I**}
Alaskan Malamute	Separation Anxiety	Moderate	Howling, excessive barking, digging, escaping, pacing, destructive behavior (scratching doors or windows)
Australian Cattle Dog	Separation Anxiety	High	Excessive barking, destructive behavior, pacing, restlessness, hypersensitivity to sounds
Australian Shepherd	Generalized Anxiety, Separation Anxiety	Medium	Excessive nipping, obsessive behaviors, restlessness, seeking reassurance, destructiveness, pacing
Beagle	Separation Anxiety	High	Excessive howling, digging, destructive behavior, pacing, restlessness, trying to escape
Belgian Malinois	Separation Anxiety	High	Excessive barking, destructive behavior (chewing furniture or belongings), restlessness, pacing, escape attempts
Bernese Mountain Dog	Noise Anxiety, Separation Anxiety	Low	Hiding, seeking comfort, panting, pacing, restlessness, destructiveness, hypersensitivity to sounds
Bichon Frise	Social Anxiety, Separation Anxiety	Low	Excessive trembling, fearfulness, avoidance of social interactions, separation distress, seeking reassurance, destructiveness, restlessness
Border Collie	Separation Anxiety	High	Excessive herding behavior, restlessness, pacing, destructive behavior, vocalization, obsessive behaviors, hypersensitivity to sounds
Boston Terrier	Noise Anxiety, Separation Anxiety	Medium	Excessive panting, seeking comfort, restlessness, destructiveness, excessive barking, hypersensitivity to sounds
Boxer	Generalized Anxiety	High	Pacing, excessive drooling, restlessness, hyperactivity, destructive behavior, compulsive behaviors
Brittany	Noise Anxiety	Moderate	Panting, trembling, hiding, seeking comfort, restlessness, pacing, attempting to escape during loud noises or thunderstorms
Bulldog (English/French)	Social Anxiety, Separation Anxiety	Medium	Avoidance of social situations, fear of new people, separation distress, excessive drooling, destructive behavior, panting, pacing

A Must Have Guidebook for Dog Lovers

40 Popular breeds anxiety type, level, and signs, Part II

Breed Name	Anxiety Type	Anxiety Level	Anxiety Signs
Cane Corso	General Anxiety	Moderate	Excessive barking, growling, aggression, destructive behavior (chewing objects or furniture), restlessness, compulsive behaviors
Cardigan Welsh Corgi	Noise Anxiety	Low	Panting, trembling, seeking reassurance, cowering, attempting to hide, restlessness, pacing during loud noises or fireworks
Cavalier King Charles Spaniel	Separation Anxiety	Low	Excessive whining, separation distress, seeking reassurance, destructive behavior, restlessness
Chihuahua	Social Anxiety, Separation Anxiety	High	Excessive trembling, aggression, fearfulness, excessive barking, hiding, seeking reassurance, separation distress, avoidance of social interactions
Cocker Spaniel	Noise Anxiety, Separation Anxiety	Medium	Hiding, excessive barking, panting, trembling, destructiveness, restlessness, hypersensitivity to sounds
Dachshund	Separation Anxiety	Medium	Excessive whining, self-destructive behavior, restlessness, digging, trying to escape, hypersensitivity to sounds
Doberman Pinscher	Social Anxiety	High	Fearful body language, avoidance, aggression, restlessness, excessive barking, panting, trembling, hypersensitivity to sounds
English Cocker Spaniel	General Anxiety	Moderate	Excessive barking, whining, restlessness, compulsive behaviors (tail chasing, paw licking), separation anxiety, seeking constant attention
English Setter	Generalized Anxiety, Separation Anxiety	Medium	Excessive pacing, trembling, restlessness, seeking reassurance, destructive behavior, separation distress
German Shepherd	Noise Anxiety, Separation Anxiety	High	Panting, trembling, hiding, whining, excessive barking, destructiveness, trying to escape, hypersensitivity to sounds, pacing, restlessness
Golden Retriever	Generalized Anxiety, Separation Anxiety	Low	Restlessness, excessive grooming, seeking reassurance, compulsive behaviors, hypervigilance, panting, trembling

Explore the Dark Side of Dogs Life

40 Popular breeds anxiety type, level, and signs, Part III

Breed Name	Anxiety Type	Anxiety Level	Anxiety Signs
Great Dane	Noise Anxiety, Separation Anxiety	Low	Hiding, seeking comfort, panting, trembling, pacing, restlessness, hypersensitivity to sounds
Labrador Retriever	Separation Anxiety	Medium	Excessive barking, destructive behavior, pacing, drooling, attempting to escape
Leonberger	Separation Anxiety	Moderate	Excessive whining, whimpering, pacing, restlessness, destructive behavior (scratching doors or furniture), drooling
Maltese	Separation Anxiety	Low	Excessive chewing, urinating, restlessness, seeking reassurance, separation distress
Miniature Schnauzer	Separation Anxiety	Medium	Excessive barking, digging, pacing, restlessness, destructive behavior, hypersensitivity to sounds
Norwegian Elkhound	Noise Anxiety	Moderate	Howling, pacing, hiding, seeking comfort, trembling, restlessness, attempts to escape during loud noises or fireworks
Poodle (Standard/Mini/Toy)	Noise Anxiety, Separation Anxiety	Low	Shaking, seeking comfort, hiding, excessive barking, destructiveness, panting, pacing
Portuguese Water Dog	General Anxiety	Low	Excessive barking, panting, restlessness, pacing, compulsive behaviors (licking, chewing), seeking constant attention, separation anxiety
Pug	Generalized Anxiety	Low	Excessive licking, clinginess, seeking reassurance, hypervigilance, restlessness, separation distress
Rottweiler	Social Anxiety	High	Aggression, fearfulness, avoidance of social interactions, hypervigilance, restlessness, excessive barking
Shiba Inu	Noise Anxiety, Separation Anxiety	Medium	Excessive vocalization, hiding, restlessness, destructiveness, trying to escape, hypersensitivity to sounds

A Must Have Guidebook for Dog Lovers

40 Popular breeds anxiety type, level, and signs, Part IV

Breed Name	Anxiety Type	Anxiety Level	Anxiety Signs
Shih Tzu	Separation Anxiety	Low	Excessive barking, restlessness, trembling, seeking reassurance, separation distress, destructive behavior
Siberian Husky	Generalized Anxiety, Separation Anxiety	High	Excessive escape attempts, destructive behavior, howling, pacing, restlessness, digging, self-mutilation, trying to escape, hypervigilance
Staffordshire Bull Terrier	Generalized Anxiety	High	Aggression, excessive panting, restlessness, destructive behavior, separation distress, hypersensitivity to sounds
Volpino Italiano	Separation Anxiety	Low	Excessive whining, barking, destructiveness (chewing objects or furniture), clinginess, pacing, attempts to escape
Welsh Springer Spaniel	General Anxiety	Low	Excessive barking, whining, restlessness, compulsive behaviors (tail chasing, paw licking), separation anxiety, seeking constant attention
Yorkshire Terrier	Noise Anxiety, Separation Anxiety	Low	Hiding, excessive barking, trembling, panting, seeking comfort, restlessness, destructiveness

Please keep in mind that our anxiety levels can be different from one dog to another, and they can be influenced by factors like our genetics, how we were raised, and the environment around us.

The signs mentioned in the table are just general indications, and they may not apply to every dog of our breed. That's why it's so important for our loving owners to consult with a veterinarian or a professional behaviorist. They can provide a thorough assessment and give us tailored guidance that's specific to our unique needs. With their help, we can better understand and manage our anxiety, leading to a happier and more positive life.

Explore the Dark Side of Dogs Life

40 Popular breeds anxiety signs and root causes

40 Popular Breeds anxiety signs and root causes, Part I

Breed	Anxiety Signs	Root Cause
Alaskan Malamute	Excessive howling or whining, destructive behavior	Separation anxiety, lack of mental stimulation
Australian Cattle Dog	Hyperactivity, restlessness, nipping or herding behavior	Lack of physical and mental exercise, boredom
Australian Shepherd	Excessive barking, compulsive behaviors, restlessness	Lack of mental stimulation, separation anxiety
Beagle	Excessive baying, digging or escaping behavior	Boredom, lack of mental and physical exercise
Belgian Malinois	Excessive vigilance, hyperactivity, aggression	Lack of mental and physical exercise, insecurity
Bernese Mountain Dog	Excessive drooling, destructive behavior, withdrawal	Separation anxiety, fear of loud noises
Bichon Frise	Excessive barking, separation anxiety, trembling	Separation anxiety, fear of being alone
Border Collie	Obsessive behaviors, herding tendencies, pacing	Lack of mental stimulation, herding instincts
Boston Terrier	Hyperactivity, destructive chewing, excessive licking	Boredom, separation anxiety
Boxer	Jumping on people, excessive playfulness, restlessness	Lack of physical exercise, separation anxiety
Brittany	Nervousness, separation anxiety, destructive behavior	Lack of mental stimulation, fear of being alone
Bulldog (English/French)	Heavy panting, excessive drooling, avoidance behaviors	Fear of certain situations, respiratory issues
Cane Corso	Aggressive behaviors, guarding tendencies, hyperactivity	Lack of socialization, insecurity
Cardigan Welsh Corgi	Fearful behavior, excessive barking, separation anxiety	Lack of socialization, fear of being alone
Cavalier King Charles Spaniel	Shyness, submissive behavior, hiding or cowering	Lack of socialization, fear of new environments
Chihuahua	Excessive barking, trembling or shaking, aggression	Fear of strangers, fear-based aggression
Cocker Spaniel	Excessive licking, separation anxiety, fearfulness	Separation anxiety, fear of abandonment
Dachshund	Excessive barking, hiding or burrowing, aggression	Fear-based aggression, lack of socialization
Doberman Pinscher	Hypervigilance, guarding behavior, aggression	Lack of socialization, fear-based aggression
English Cocker Spaniel	Submissive urination, separation anxiety, fearfulness	Separation anxiety, fear of punishment
English Setter	Separation anxiety, destructive behavior, restlessness	Lack of mental and physical exercise, boredom
German Shepherd	Excessive barking, pacing, hyper-vigilance	Lack of mental and physical exercise, insecurity

A Must Have Guidebook for Dog Lovers

40 Popular Breeds anxiety signs and root causes, Part II

Breed	Anxiety Signs	Root Cause
Golden Retriever	Excessive chewing, attention-seeking behavior	Separation anxiety, lack of mental stimulation
Great Dane	Shyness, fearfulness, separation anxiety	Lack of socialization, fear of new environments
Labrador Retriever	Excessive chewing, hyperactivity, restlessness	Lack of mental and physical exercise, boredom
Leonberger	Separation anxiety, clingy behavior, destructive chewing	Lack of mental stimulation, fear of being alone
Maltese	Excessive barking, trembling or shaking, hiding	Separation anxiety, fear of new environments
Miniature Schnauzer	Aggression towards strangers, excessive barking	Fear of strangers, fear-based aggression
Norwegian Elkhound	Destructive behavior, excessive howling or barking	Separation anxiety, boredom
Poodle (Standard/Mini/Toy)	Clinginess, separation anxiety, restlessness	Lack of mental stimulation, fear of being alone
Portuguese Water Dog	Excessive barking, destructive behavior, hyperactivity	Lack of mental and physical exercise, boredom
Pug	Heavy panting, wheezing, difficulty breathing	Respiratory issues, separation anxiety
Rottweiler	Aggressive behaviors, guarding tendencies, fearfulness	Lack of socialization, fear-based aggression
Shiba Inu	Fearful behavior, aggression towards strangers	Fear of strangers, fear-based aggression
Shih Tzu	Excessive barking, separation anxiety, clinginess	Separation anxiety, fear of being alone
Siberian Husky	Excessive howling, destructive behavior, escapism	Boredom, separation anxiety
Staffordshire Bull Terrier	Aggression towards other dogs, hyperactivity	Fear-based aggression, lack of socialization
Volpino Italiano	Excessive barking, restlessness, destructive behavior	Separation anxiety, fear of being alone
Welsh Springer Spaniel	Fearful behavior, separation anxiety, excessive licking	Lack of socialization, fear of being alone
Yorkshire Terrier	Excessive barking, shyness, aggression	Fear-based aggression, lack of socialization

Please note that this table provides general information and that individual dogs may vary in their anxiety signs and root causes. <u>It's important to consult with a veterinarian or a professional dog behaviorist</u> for a comprehensive evaluation and personalized guidance if you suspect your dog is experiencing anxiety.

Explore the Dark Side of Dogs Life

40 Popular breeds hygiene detail

40 Popular breeds hygiene detail, Part I

Breed	Grooming Needs	Coat Type	Shedding Level	Frequency	Brushing	Bathing	Trimming
Alaskan Malamute	High	Double	High	Regular	Daily	Monthly	Occasional
Australian Cattle Dog	Low	Short	Moderate	Regular	Weekly	Monthly	As needed
Australian Shepherd	Moderate	Medium/Long	Moderate	Regular	Weekly	Monthly	Occasional
Beagle	Low	Short	Low	Regular	Weekly	Monthly	As needed
Belgian Malinois	Moderate	Short	Moderate	Regular	Weekly	Monthly	As needed
Bernese Mountain Dog	High	Long	High	Regular	Daily	Monthly	Occasional
Bichon Frise	High	Curly	Low	Regular	Daily	Monthly	Regularly
Border Collie	Moderate	Medium/Long	Moderate	Regular	Weekly	Monthly	Occasional
Boston Terrier	Low	Short	Low	Regular	Weekly	Monthly	As needed
Boxer	Low	Short	Low	Regular	Weekly	Monthly	As needed
Brittany	Moderate	Medium	Moderate	Regular	Weekly	Monthly	Occasional
Bulldog (English/French)	Low	Short	Low	Regular	Weekly	Monthly	As needed
Cane Corso	Low	Short	Low	Regular	Weekly	Monthly	As needed
Cardigan Welsh Corgi	Moderate	Medium	Moderate	Regular	Weekly	Monthly	Occasional
Cavalier King Charles Spaniel	Moderate	Medium/Long	Moderate	Regular	Weekly	Monthly	Occasional
Chihuahua	Low	Short	Low	Regular	Weekly	Monthly	As needed
Cocker Spaniel	High	Medium/Long	High	Regular	Daily	Monthly	Regularly
Dachshund	Low	Short	Low	Regular	Weekly	Monthly	As needed
Doberman Pinscher	Low	Short	Low	Regular	Weekly	Monthly	As needed
English Cocker Spaniel	High	Medium/Long	High	Regular	Daily	Monthly	Regularly
English Setter	High	Long	High	Regular	Daily	Monthly	Regularly
German Shepherd	Moderate	Medium/Long	Moderate	Regular	Weekly	Monthly	Occasional
Golden Retriever	High	Long	High	Regular	Daily	Monthly	Occasional
Great Dane	Low	Short	Low	Regular	Weekly	Monthly	As needed

A Must Have Guidebook for Dog Lovers

40 Popular breeds hygiene detail, Part II

Breed	Grooming Needs	Coat Type	Shedding Level	Frequency	Brushing	Bathing	Trimming
Labrador Retriever	Low	Short	Low	Regular	Weekly	Monthly	As needed
Leonberger	High	Long	High	Regular	Daily	Monthly	Occasional
Maltese	High	Long	Low	Regular	Daily	Monthly	Regularly
Miniature Schnauzer	High	Wire-haired	Low	Regular	Daily	Monthly	Regularly
Norwegian Elkhound	Moderate	Short	Moderate	Regular	Weekly	Monthly	As needed
Poodle (Standard/Mini/Toy)	High	Curly	Low	Regular	Daily	Monthly	Regularly
Portuguese Water Dog	High	Curly	Low	Regular	Daily	Monthly	Regularly
Pug	Low	Short	Low	Regular	Daily	Monthly	As needed
Rottweiler	Low	Short	Low	Regular	Weekly	Monthly	As needed
Shiba Inu	Moderate	Double	Moderate	Regular	Weekly	Monthly	As needed
Shih Tzu	High	Long	Low	Regular	Daily	Monthly	Regularly
Siberian Husky	Moderate	Medium	High	Regular	Weekly	Monthly	Occasional
Staffordshire Bull Terrier	Low	Short	Low	Regular	Weekly	Monthly	As needed
Volpino Italiano	Moderate	Double	Moderate	Regular	Weekly	Monthly	As needed
Welsh Springer Spaniel	Moderate	Medium/Long	Moderate	Regular	Weekly	Monthly	Occasional
Yorkshire Terrier	High	Long	Low	Regular	Daily	Monthly	Regularly

Please note that the table provides a general overview and individual dogs may have specific grooming needs that could vary. It's always a good idea to consult breed-specific grooming guidelines or consult a professional groomer for personalized advice.

Explore the Dark Side of Dogs Life

40 Popular breeds training aspects

40 popular breeds training aspects table, Part I

Breed Name	Trainability	Intelligence	Exercise Needs	Socialization Needs	Training Tips
Alaskan Malamute	Moderate	High	High	High	Use positive reinforcement and consistency in training
Australian Cattle Dog	High	High	High	High	Provide mental stimulation and regular exercise
Australian Shepherd	High	High	High	High	Focus on mental and physical activities for training
Beagle	Moderate	Moderate	Moderate	High	Use rewards and treats for motivation in training
Belgian Malinois	High	High	High	High	Channel their energy into structured training sessions
Bernese Mountain Dog	Moderate	Average	Moderate	Moderate	Use positive reinforcement and gentle training methods
Bichon Frise	Moderate	High	Moderate	High	Use positive reinforcement and consistency in training
Border Collie	High	High	High	High	Provide mental and physical challenges in training
Boston Terrier	Moderate	Average	Moderate	Moderate	Use positive reinforcement and consistency in training
Boxer	Moderate	Average	High	High	Start training early and use positive reinforcement
Brittany	High	Average	High	High	Provide mental and physical exercise for training
Bulldog (English/French)	Low	Average	Low	Moderate	Use positive reinforcement and patience in training
Cane Corso	Moderate	High	High	High	Establish consistent rules and boundaries in training
Cardigan Welsh Corgi	High	High	Moderate	High	Use positive reinforcement and mental stimulation

A Must Have Guidebook for Dog Lovers

40 popular breeds training aspects table, Part II

Breed Name	Trainability	Intelligence	Exercise Needs	Socialization Needs	Training Tips
Cavalier King Charles Spaniel	Moderate	Average	Moderate	High	Use rewards and positive reinforcement in training
Chihuahua	Low	Average	Low	Moderate	Use gentle training methods and positive reinforcement
Cocker Spaniel	Moderate	Average	Moderate	High	Provide mental stimulation and positive reinforcement
Dachshund	Moderate	Average	Moderate	Moderate	Be patient and consistent in training
Doberman Pinscher	High	High	High	High	Provide consistent training and positive reinforcement
English Cocker Spaniel	Moderate	Average	Moderate	High	Use positive reinforcement and consistency in training
English Setter	Moderate	Average	Moderate	High	Use positive reinforcement and mental stimulation
German Shepherd	High	High	High	High	Provide consistent training and mental stimulation
Golden Retriever	High	High	High	High	Use positive reinforcement and consistency in training
Great Dane	Low	Average	Moderate	Moderate	Start training early and use gentle training methods
Labrador Retriever	High	High	High	High	Use positive reinforcement and consistency in training
Leonberger	Moderate	High	High	High	Use positive reinforcement and socialization training
Maltese	Moderate	Average	Low	High	Use positive reinforcement and be patient in training
Miniature Schnauzer	Moderate	High	Moderate	High	Use positive reinforcement and consistency in training

Explore the Dark Side of Dogs Life

40 popular breeds training aspects table, Part III

Breed Name	Trainability	Intelligence	Exercise Needs	Socialization Needs	Training Tips
Norwegian Elkhound	Moderate	Average	High	High	Start training early and provide mental stimulation
Poodle (Standard/Mini/Toy)	High	High	Moderate	High	Use positive reinforcement and mental stimulation
Portuguese Water Dog	High	High	High	High	Provide mental and physical exercise for training
Pug	Low	Average	Low	Moderate	Use positive reinforcement and be patient in training
Rottweiler	Moderate	High	High	High	Establish consistent leadership and boundaries
Shiba Inu	Moderate	Average	High	Moderate	Use positive reinforcement and consistency in training
Shih Tzu	Low	Average	Low	Moderate	Use rewards and positive reinforcement in training
Siberian Husky	Moderate	High	High	High	Use positive reinforcement and provide ample exercise
Staffordshire Bull Terrier	Moderate	Average	High	High	Use positive reinforcement and consistency in training
Volpino Italiano	Moderate	High	Moderate	High	Use positive reinforcement and socialization training
Welsh Springer Spaniel	High	Average	High	High	Provide mental and physical exercise for training
Yorkshire Terrier	Moderate	Average	Low	Moderate	Use positive reinforcement and consistency in training

Please note that trainability, intelligence, exercise needs, socialization needs, and training tips can vary within each breed, and individual dogs may have unique characteristics and requirements. This table provides a general overview to guide owners in training their dogs effectively.
<u>Also remember, dear owner, training should be a fun and engaging experience for both of us.</u> Keep the sessions short, interactive, and filled with love.

A Must Have Guidebook for Dog Lovers

Chapter 17

40 Popular breeds general health and age data

40 Popular breeds General health and age data, Part I

Breed	Common Health Issues / Predispositions	Average Lifespan	Energy Level	Recommended Vaccinations	Preventive Care
Alaskan Malamute	Hip Dysplasia, Chondrodysplasia, Cataracts	10-14 years	High	Regular check-ups	Regular exercise, mental stimulation, joint supplements
Australian Cattle Dog	Hip Dysplasia, Progressive Retinal Atrophy	12-15 years	Very High	Preventive vaccinations	Regular exercise, mental stimulation, training
Australian Shepherd	Hip Dysplasia, Collie Eye Anomaly, Epilepsy	12-15 years	High	Routine veterinary care	Regular exercise, mental stimulation, obedience training
Beagle	Intervertebral Disc Disease, Epilepsy	12-15 years	Moderate	Preventive vaccinations	Regular exercise, mental stimulation, weight management
Belgian Malinois	Hip Dysplasia, Progressive Retinal Atrophy	10-12 years	Very High	Regular check-ups	Regular exercise, mental stimulation, obedience training
Bernese Mountain Dog	Hip Dysplasia, Elbow Dysplasia, Cancer	7-10 years	Moderate	Preventive vaccinations	Regular exercise, joint supplements, regular check-ups
Bichon Frise	Patellar Luxation, Allergies	14-16 years	Moderate	Routine veterinary care	Regular grooming, dental hygiene, proper nutrition
Border Collie	Hip Dysplasia, Collie Eye Anomaly, Epilepsy	12-15 years	Very High	Preventive vaccinations	Regular exercise, mental stimulation, obedience training
Boston Terrier	Brachycephalic Syndrome, Patellar Luxation	11-13 years	Moderate	Regular veterinary care	Regular exercise, dental hygiene, weight management
Boxer	Hip Dysplasia, Boxer Cardiomyopathy	10-12 years	High	Preventive vaccinations	Regular exercise, mental stimulation, regular check-ups
Brittany	Hip Dysplasia, Epilepsy	12-14 years	High	Routine veterinary care	Regular exercise, mental stimulation, obedience training
Bulldog (English / French)	Brachycephalic Syndrome, Hip Dysplasia	8-10 years	Low to Moderate	Regular check-ups	Regular exercise, dental hygiene, weight management
Cane Corso	Hip Dysplasia, Dilated Cardiomyopathy	9-12 years	Moderate	Preventive vaccinations	Regular exercise, mental stimulation, regular check-ups
Cardigan Welsh Corgi	Progressive Retinal Atrophy, Intervertebral Disc Disease	12-15 years	Moderate	Preventive vaccinations	Regular exercise, mental stimulation, weight management

A Must Have Guidebook for Dog Lovers

40 Popular breeds General health and age data, Part II

Breed	Common Health Issues / Predispositions	Average Lifespan	Energy Level	Recommended Vaccinations	Preventive Care
Cocker Spaniel	Progressive Retinal Atrophy, Hip Dysplasia	12-15 years	Moderate	Preventive vaccinations	Regular exercise, mental stimulation, regular check-ups
Dachshund	Intervertebral Disc Disease, Patellar Luxation	12-16 years	Moderate	Routine veterinary care	Regular exercise, mental stimulation, weight management
Doberman Pinscher	Dilated Cardiomyopathy, Wobbler Syndrome	10-13 years	High	Preventive vaccinations	Regular exercise, mental stimulation, obedience training
English Cocker Spaniel	Hip Dysplasia, Progressive Retinal Atrophy	12-14 years	Moderate	Routine veterinary care	Regular exercise, mental stimulation, regular check-ups
English Setter	Hip Dysplasia, Hypothyroidism	10-12 years	Moderate	Preventive vaccinations	Regular exercise, mental stimulation, regular check-ups
German Shepherd	Hip Dysplasia, Degenerative Myelopathy	9-13 years	High	Preventive vaccinations	Regular exercise, mental stimulation, obedience training
Golden Retriever	Hip Dysplasia, Lymphoma, Progressive Retinal Atrophy	10-12 years	High	Routine veterinary care	Regular exercise, mental stimulation, regular check-ups
Great Dane	Dilated Cardiomyopathy, Gastric Dilatation-Volvulus	6-8 years	Low	Preventive vaccinations	Regular exercise, mental stimulation, regular check-ups
Leonberger	Hip Dysplasia, Osteosarcoma	8-10 years	Moderate	Regular veterinary care	Regular exercise, mental stimulation, joint supplements
Maltese	Patellar Luxation, Portosystemic Shunt	12-15 years	Low	Routine veterinary visits	Regular grooming, dental hygiene, weight management

Explore the Dark Side of Dogs Life

40 Popular breeds General health and age data, Part III

Breed	Common Health Issues / Predispositions	Average Lifespan	Energy Level	Recommended Vaccinations	Preventive Care
Miniature Schnauzer	Progressive Retinal Atrophy, Pancreatitis	12-15 years	Moderate	Preventive vaccinations	Regular exercise, mental stimulation, regular check-ups
Norwegian Elkhound	Hip Dysplasia, Progressive Retinal Atrophy	12-15 years	Moderate	Routine veterinary care	Regular exercise, mental stimulation, weight management
Poodle (Standard/Mini/Toy)	Hip Dysplasia, Progressive Retinal Atrophy	10-18 years	High	Preventive vaccinations	Regular exercise, mental stimulation, regular check-ups
Portuguese Water Dog	Hip Dysplasia, Progressive Retinal Atrophy	10-14 years	Moderate	Preventive vaccinations	Regular exercise, mental stimulation, regular check-ups
Pug	Brachycephalic Syndrome, Patellar Luxation	12-15 years	Low	Regular veterinary care	Regular exercise, dental hygiene, weight management
Shiba Inu	Patellar Luxation, Allergies	12-15 years	Moderate	Regular check-ups	Regular exercise, mental stimulation, dental hygiene
Shih Tzu	Brachycephalic Syndrome, Patellar Luxation	10-18 years	Low to Moderate	Routine veterinary care	Regular grooming, dental hygiene, weight management
Siberian Husky	Hip Dysplasia, Progressive Retinal Atrophy	12-14 years	High	Preventive vaccinations	Regular exercise, mental stimulation, regular check-ups
Staffordshire Bull Terrier	L-2-Hydroxyglutaric Aciduria, Patellar Luxation	12-14 years	High	Preventive vaccinations	Regular exercise, mental stimulation, regular check-ups
Volpino Italiano	Patellar Luxation, Progressive Retinal Atrophy	14-16 years	Moderate	Routine veterinary care	Regular exercise, mental stimulation, regular check-ups

A Must Have Guidebook for Dog Lovers

40 Popular breeds General health and age data, Part IV

Breed	Common Health Issues / Predispositions	Average Lifespan	Energy Level	Recommended Vaccinations	Preventive Care
Welsh Springer Spaniel	Hip Dysplasia, Progressive Retinal Atrophy	12-15 years	Moderate	Preventive vaccinations	Regular exercise, mental stimulation, regular check-ups
Yorkshire Terrier	Portosystemic Shunt, Tracheal Collapse	12-15 years	Low to Moderate	Routine veterinary visits	Regular exercise, dental hygiene, weight management

Please note that trainability, intelligence, exercise needs, socialization needs, and training tips can vary within each breed, and individual dogs may have unique characteristics and requirements. This table provides a general overview to guide owners in training their dogs effectively.

Also remember, dear owner, training should be a fun and engaging experience for both of us. Keep the sessions short, interactive, and filled with love.

Explore the Dark Side of Dogs Life

40 Popular breeds physiology data

40 Popular breeds physiology data, Part I					
Breed	**Size**	**Height (cm)**	**Weight (kg)**	**Coat**
Alaskan Malamute	Large	61 - 66	Male: 38-50 Female: 34-40	Thick, double coat
Australian Cattle Dog	Medium	43 - 51	Male: 15-22 Female: 14-20	Short, dense coat
Australian Shepherd	Medium-Large	46 - 58	Male: 25-32 Female: 16-32	Medium-length, double coat
Beagle	Small-Medium	33 - 41	41852	Short, sleek coat
Belgian Malinois	Medium-Large	61 - 66	Male: 25-30 Female: 22-25	Short, dense coat
Bernese Mountain Dog	Large	58 - 70	Male: 45-50 Female: 38-50	Long, thick, wavy coat
Bichon Frise	Small-Medium	23 - 30	Male: 3-5.5 Female: 3-5	Curly, dense coat
Border Collie	Medium	46 - 53	Male: 14-20 Female: 12-15	Medium-length, double coat
Boston Terrier	Small-Medium	38 - 43	Male: 5-11 Female: 4-7	Short, smooth coat
Boxer	Medium-Large	53 - 63	Male: 25-32 Female: 22-29	Short, smooth coat
Brittany	Medium	43 - 52	Male: 14-18, Female: 12.5-15.5	Medium-length, wavy coat
Bulldog (English/French)	Medium	31 - 40	Male 22-25 Female 18-23	Short, smooth coat
Cane Corso	Large	64 - 68	Male: 45-50 Female: 40-45	Short, dense coat
Cardigan Welsh Corgi	Small-Medium	25 - 31	Male: 12-17 Female: 11-15	Medium-length, dense coat
Cavalier King Charles Spaniel	Small-Medium	30 - 33	Male & Female 5-9	Long, silky coat
Chihuahua	Tiny-Small	15 - 23	Male & Female 1.5-3	Short, smooth coat
Cocker Spaniel	Medium	36 - 41	Male: 12-16 Female: 11-14	Medium-length, silky coat
Dachshund	Small-Medium	13 - 23	Male & Female 5-12	Short, smooth coat
Doberman Pinscher	Large	63 - 72	Male: 34-45 Female: 27-41	Short, smooth coat
English Cocker Spaniel	Medium	38 - 43	Male: 13-1 Female: 12-15	Medium-length, silky coat
English Setter	Medium-Large	61 - 69	Male: 25-36 Female: 20-30	Long, silky coat
German Shepherd	Large	55 - 65	Male: 30-40 Female: 22-32	Double coat with dense undercoat

A Must Have Guidebook for Dog Lovers

40 Popular breeds physiology data, Part II

Breed	Size	Height (cm)	Weight (kg)	Coat
Golden Retriever	Large	51 - 61	Male: 29-34 Female: 25-32	Dense, water-repellent coat
Great Dane	Large-Giant	71 - 86	Male: 54-90 Female: 45-59	Short, smooth coat
Labrador Retriever	Large	55 - 62	Male: 29-36 Female: 25-32	Short, dense coat
Leonberger	Large-Giant	65 - 80	Male: 54-77 Female: 41-54	Dense, water-resistant coat
Maltese	Tiny-Small	20 - 25	Male: 5.5-8 Female: 4.5-6.5	Long, silky coat
Miniature Schnauzer	Small-Medium	30 - 36	Male: 5-8, Female: 4-6	Double coat with wiry topcoat
Norwegian Elkhound	Medium	48 - 53	Male: 23–28 Female: 18–23	Double coat with dense undercoat
Poodle (Standard/Mini/Toy)	Small-Large	24 - 60	Std: Male: 18-32 Female: 18-27 Miniature: Male: 4-6 Female: 3.5-5 Toy: Male: 2-4 Female: 2-3	Curly, hypoallergenic coat
Portuguese Water Dog	Medium-Large	43 - 57	Male: 19-27 Female: 16-23	Curly, water-resistant coat
Pug	Small-Medium	25 - 36	Male: 6-9 Female 5-8	Short, smooth coat
Rottweiler	Large	56 - 69	Male: 50-60, Female: 35-48	Short, dense coat
Shiba Inu	Medium	35 - 43	Male: 10–11 Female: 8–9	Double coat with straight outercoat
Shih Tzu	Small	20 - 28	Male and Female 4-9	Long, flowing coat
Siberian Husky	Medium-Large	50 - 60	Male: 20-28 Female: 16-23	Thick, double coat
Staffordshire Bull Terrier	Medium	35 - 40	Male: 13–17 Female: 11–16	Short, smooth coat
Volpino Italiano	Small	26 - 30	Male: 4-5 Female 3-4	Dense, double coat
Welsh Springer Spaniel	Medium	46 - 48	Male: 20-25 Female: 16-20	Medium-length, wavy coat
Yorkshire Terrier	Tiny-Small	17 - 23	Male and Female 2-3	Long, silky coat

Kindly be aware that the information provided is general and may vary among individual pups, even within the same breed. It is essential to consult a veterinarian or an expert for personalized advice tailored to your specific dog Details.

Explore the Dark Side of Dogs Life

40 Popular breeds intelligence level

40 Popular breeds intelligence level, Part I	
Tier 1: The brightest dogs	Dogs in this tier are considered the most intelligent and able to learn a new command in fewer than 5 repetitions. They also tend to understand new commands quickly and can generalize commands to new situations.
Tier 2: Excellent working dogs	Dogs in this tier are highly intelligent and able to learn a new command in fewer than 5-15 repetitions. They tend to understand new commands quickly and can generalize commands to new situations.
Tier 3: Above-average working dogs	Dogs in this tier are considered above average in terms of intelligence and can learn a new command in fewer than 15-25 repetitions. They may require more repetition to understand new commands but are still able to generalize commands to new situations.
Tier 4: Average working dogs	Dogs in this tier are considered average in terms of intelligence and can learn a new command in fewer than 25-40 repetitions. They may require more repetition to understand new commands and may have difficulty generalizing commands to new situations.
Tier 5: Fair working dogs	Dogs in this tier are considered fair in terms of intelligence and can learn a new command in fewer than 40-80 repetitions. They may have difficulty understanding new commands and may require more repetition to learn them.
Tier 6: Lowest degree of working	Dogs in this tier are considered the least intelligent and may have difficulty learning new commands, understanding them, or generalizing them to new situations. They may require more than 100 repetitions to learn a new command.

Breed	Tier 1	Tier 2	Tier 3	Tier 4	Tier 5	Tier 6
Alaskan Malamute						20%
Australian Cattle		85%				
Australian Shepherd		85%				
Beagle						30%
Belgian Malinois			30%			
Bernese Mountain					50%	
Bichon Frise						25%
Border Collie	95%					
Boston Terrier						40%
Boxer				50%		
Brittany			30%			
Bulldog (English/French)						40%
Cane Corso						30%

A Must Have Guidebook for Dog Lovers

40 Popular breeds intelligence level, Part II

Breed	Tier 1	Tier 2	Tier 3	Tier 4	Tier 5	Tier 6
Cardigan Welsh Corgi						80%
Cavalier King Charles Spaniel						50%
Chihuahua						30%
Cocker Spaniel						30%
Dachshund						25%
Doberman Pinscher	85%					
English Cocker Spaniel						50%
English Setter						40%
German Shepherd	95%					
Golden Retriever	95%					
Great Dane						25%
Labrador Retriever				85%		
Leonberger						50%
Maltese						50%
Miniature Schnauzer						50%
Norwegian Elkhound						30%
Poodle (Standard/Mini/Toy)	95%					
Portuguese Water						50%
Pug						25%
Rottweiler				85%		
Shiba Inu						40%
Shih Tzu						70%
Siberian Husky					85%	
Staffordshire Bull Terrier						40%
Volpino Italiano						No data
Welsh Springer Spaniel			50%			
Yorkshire Terrier						30%

Please note that intelligence can be measured in different ways, and this is just one ranking based on a specific set of criteria. Additionally, each individual dog is unique and may exhibit its own intelligence and problem-solving abilities regardless of breed.

40 Popular breeds nap, walk, and in/outdoor profile

Breed	Sleep Hours	Daily Walk Hours	Exercise Needs	Indoor/Outdoor
Alaskan Malamute	14-16	2-3	High	Outdoor
Australian Cattle Dog	12-14	2-3	High	Outdoor
Australian Shepherd	12-14	2-3	High	Outdoor
Beagle	12-14	1-2	Moderate	Both
Belgian Malinois	12-14	2-3	High	Outdoor
Bernese Mountain Dog	14-16	2-3	Moderate	Outdoor
Bichon Frise	14-16	1-2	Moderate	Indoor
Border Collie	12-14	2-3	High	Outdoor
Boston Terrier	12-14	1-2	Moderate	Both
Boxer	12-14	1-2	High	Indoor
Brittany	12-14	2-3	High	Outdoor
Bulldog (English/French)	14-16	1-2	Low	Indoor
Cane Corso	12-14	1-2	Moderate	Both
Cardigan Welsh Corgi	12-14	1-2	Moderate	Indoor
Cavalier King Charles Spaniel	12-14	1-2	Moderate	Indoor
Chihuahua	14-16	1	Low	Indoor
Cocker Spaniel	12-14	1-2	Moderate	Both
Dachshund	12-14	1-2	Moderate	Both
Doberman Pinscher	12-14	2-3	High	Outdoor
English Cocker Spaniel	12-14	2-3	Moderate	Both
English Setter	12-14	2-3	Moderate	Outdoor
German Shepherd	12-14	2-3	High	Outdoor
Golden Retriever	12-14	2-3	High	Outdoor
Great Dane	14-16	1-2	Low	Indoor
Labrador Retriever	12-14	2-3	High	Outdoor
Leonberger	12-14	2-3	Moderate	Outdoor
Maltese	14-16	1-2	Low	Indoor
Miniature Schnauzer	12-14	1-2	Moderate	Indoor
Norwegian Elkhound	12-14	1-2	Moderate	Both
Poodle (Standard/Mini/Toy)	12-14	1-2	Moderate	Indoor

A Must Have Guidebook for Dog Lovers

40 Popular breeds nap, walk and in/outdoor profile, Part II				
Breed	Sleep Hours	Daily Walk Hours	Exercise Needs	Indoor/Outdoor
Portuguese Water Dog	12-14	2-3	High	Both
Pug	14-16	1-2	Low	Indoor
Rottweiler	12-14	2-3	High	Outdoor
Shiba Inu	14-16	1-2	Moderate	Both
Shih Tzu	14-16	1-2	Low	Indoor
Siberian Husky	14-16	2-3	High	Outdoor
Staffordshire Bull Terrier	12-14	2-3	High	Both
Volpino Italiano	12-14	1-2	Moderate	Indoor
Welsh Springer Spaniel	12-14	2-3	High	Outdoor
Yorkshire Terrier	14-16	1-2	Low	Indoor

Remember that these are general guidelines and individual dogs may have slightly different needs based on their age, health, and overall energy levels. Always consult with a veterinarian to ensure you meet your furry friend's specific requirements. Happy snoozing and wagging!

Explore the Dark Side of Dogs Life

Puppy life stage development

Puppy life stage development table

Age (Weeks)	Physical Development	Behavioral Development	Training Milestones	Health Care	Feeding Schedule	Potty Training	Socialization
1-2	Eyes and ears open	Crawling, limited mobility	None	First visit to the veterinarian	Frequent nursing from mother	Not yet initiated	Early exposure to gentle human touch
3-4	Starting to walk	Developing senses and awareness	Introduction to basic commands	Vaccination schedule begins	Transition to soft puppy food	Begin introducing puppy pads or outdoor area	Gentle introduction to other animals
5-6	First baby teeth emerge	Curiosity and exploration	Housebreaking training begins	Continue vaccinations	Regular meals with puppy food	Consistent potty-training routine	Positive experiences with new people
7-8	Adult teeth start to come in	Increased mobility and playfulness	Introduction to leash and collar	Regular check-ups and deworming	Scheduled meals with appropriate portions	Reinforce potty training consistency	Exposure to various environments
9-12	Growth spurt	Improved coordination and balance	Advanced obedience training	Spaying neutering considerations	Scheduled meals with appropriate portions	Refine potty training skills	Continued socialization with humans animals
13-16	Adolescent phase	Sexual maturity	Advanced obedience training	Dental care, flea tick prevention	Regular meals with appropriate portions	Reinforce potty training consistency	Continued exposure to new experiences
17-20	Fully developed body	Behavioral maturity and independence	Advanced commands and tricks	Regular health check-ups and vaccinations	Regular meals with appropriate portions	Consistent reinforcement of potty training	Maintain positive social interactions
20+	- Adult dog	Full maturity	Continued advanced training	Regular grooming and preventive care	Regular meals with appropriate portions	Reinforce good potty habits	Ongoing socialization and mental stimulation

This table provides a general timeline and general guide to help new puppy owners keep track of essential aspects of care and development. However, it's important to note every puppy is unique and each individual puppies may have unique needs and variations. <u>Consult with your veterinarian for specific vaccination schedules and dietary recommendations tailored to your puppy's breed, size, and health requirements.</u>

Remember, this table serves as a starting point, and your puppy's journey will be filled with exciting discoveries and adjustments along the way. Enjoy the adventure of raising a happy and healthy pup! Woof!

A Must Have Guidebook for Dog Lovers

Glossary

Woof woof! Let me share with you some popular terms that make us dogs wag our tails with delight. These words are like our secret code for having awesome interactions with you. So, if you come across a word in the book that makes you go <u>Huh?</u> – just flip to the Glossary, and you'll find what it means! It's like our way of helping you learn our language, and trust me, it'll make our time together even more paw-some!

Adopt: The act of welcoming a homeless or abandoned dog into a loving forever home, giving them a second chance at happiness.

Backup: When you say this, I know it's time to take a few steps backward.

Bark: Our way of speaking up, whether it's to protect our territory or to get your attention.

Barking mad: When we're feeling extra playful and full of energy, it's our way of letting you know we're ready for some excitement.

Belly rub: Like a canine massage, it's pure bliss that makes us melt with happiness.

Best friend: The special human who holds a special place in our hearts, offering love, companionship, and endless adventures.

Butt Wiggle: Oh, this one is hilarious! My back end wiggles while my front legs stay put. It's like a pre-wag warm-up, meaning I'm bursting with joy!

Crawl: A fun trick where I move forward really low, like a sneaky crawl.

Cuddle: The heartwarming act of snuggling up close to our humans, creating a bond of love and warmth.

Down: It means I should lie down on my belly, all ready for cuddles or a treat.

Go Boop: That's when you gently tap my nose – it's like a little hello!

Explore the Dark Side of Dogs Life

Glossary

Good boy/girl: The words we love to hear from our humans, praising us for our good behavior and making us feel loved and appreciated.

Grooming: The process of keeping our fur clean and looking fabulous, whether it's through brushing, bathing, or getting a trim.

Happy Helicopter: Imagine my tail spinning like a helicopter rotor. Yep, that's a Happy Helicopter! It happens when I'm super-duper thrilled or eagerly awaiting something fun.

Hide: Oh, the hide-and-seek game! I love finding you, and treats too!

Hug: When you put your arms around me, I feel your love and warmth.

Leash: Our trusty companion that keeps us safe and connected to our humans during our adventures.

Naptime: Our favorite pastime is curling up in a cozy spot and recharging our batteries with a blissful snooze.

Nervous Nudge: When I'm a bit uncertain or a tad anxious, my tail gives a quick, hesitant wag. It's my way of saying, "I'm not entirely sure about this, but I'm trying!"

Paw: It's my way of giving you a high-five or asking for treats.

Playdate: A fun-filled get-together with our fellow furry friends, where we can romp, chase, and have a tail-wagging good time.

Rescue: The heroic act of saving a dog from a difficult or unsafe situation, providing them with love, care, and a forever home.

Roll Over: A playful command to flip on my back – belly rub time!

Sniff: Our superpower sense of smell that allows us to explore and discover the world around us.

A Must Have Guidebook for Dog Lovers

Chapter 17

Snuggle buddy: A furry friend or a human who loves to cuddle and snuggle with us, providing comfort and warmth.

Snuggle buddy: A furry friend or a human who loves to cuddle and snuggle with us, providing comfort and warmth.

Tail Flagging: I hold my tail high and wave it gently from side to side, showing off my confidence and positive vibes. I'm feeling great!

Tail-Twist: Is when my tail does a little dance, showing how excited and happy I am to see you!

Touch: When you say this, I know to press my nose against your hand.

Training: The process of learning new skills and behaviors through positive reinforcement, helping us become well-behaved and obedient companions.

Treat time: The much-anticipated moment when we get rewarded with tasty snacks for being good boys and girls.

Treat: The ultimate reward for being the best furry companion, a tasty delight that we can't resist.

Vet: Oh, the vet is our furry doctor! They take care of our health and well-being. Visiting the vet regularly for check-ups, vaccinations, and any health concerns is important. They help keep us healthy and happy.

Wags:

Full-Body Wag: Brace yourself for this one! I can't contain my excitement, so my entire body joins the wag party. It's pure happiness unleashed!

Happy Sniff Wag: Oh boy, when I'm sniffing something fascinating, my tail can't help but wag in excitement! It's like saying, "This smells amazing! Let's explore!"

Slow Wag: Sometimes, I wag my tail slowly and carefully. It's like I'm saying, "I'm curious, but I'm taking my time to figure things out."

Subtle Wag: Sometimes, I give a gentle wag, just a little movement of my tail. It shows that I'm content and peaceful in the moment.

Tail wag: The legendary expression of joy and happiness, a wag that says we love you.

Explore the Dark Side of Dogs Life

Glossary

Wait: This one's important – it means I should pause and be patient for your next cue.

Walk: Music to our ears means we get to explore the world and exercise alongside our favorite human.

Walkies: The exciting adventure of going for a walk with our humans, exploring the neighborhood, sniffing new scents, and enjoying the great outdoors.

Wave: I lift my paw to say hello or goodbye, just like a friendly wave!

Zoomies: Those bursts of pure joy and energy that make us sprint around in circles or zigzag through the house or yard

A Must Have Guidebook for Dog Lovers

Dog-book Logbook

Dog-book Logbook

A Must Have Guidebook for Dog Lovers

Dog-book Logbook

From Worries to Wags

Explore the Dark Side of Dogs Life

Dog-book Logbook

English Edition

A Must Have Guidebook for Dog Lovers

Dog-book Logbook

Explore the Dark Side of Dogs Life

www.ingramcontent.com/pod-product-compliance
Lightning Source LLC
Chambersburg PA
CBHW051426290426
44109CB00016B/1448